AW SHIT.... I JUST WOKE UP.
ANYWAYS, I AM THE NARRATOR
OF THIS SHIT BUK HE KEPT ME
AWAKE A COUPLE OF NIGHTS
CRACKED OUT OF~ EXCITMENT

HENCE

WHY I WOKE UP
LATE. FUK YOU
I DONT GET PAID ENOUGH
FOR THIS.~..

PAST THIS POINT YOU WILL SEE HIS ART
GOODBYE FOR NOW

~~2017~~ 2018 ~~2019~~ was a pretty ~~XXXX~~ Nightmarish moment in life. It always takes me forever to get acustomed to new envirnments.

I got stuck being home

STUCK IN My own head. depressed with what shit was happening in that time.

So I just kept drawing. At home not really socializing, not even with my family.

Is when I started community college. noone to talk to. ~~noone to notice~~

I started talking to more people lifes turning for the Better. Scared itll all happen again. Everyone will leave ~~noone likes~~

Think Better thoughts you need to clear out the negativity. All that Bad Energy

I HATE THIS FEELING.
I KNOW ITS ALL IN MY HEAD.
Just that feeling that people hate me keeps getting stronger. but then dies down. Ive been feeling it for a bit now

I DON'T KNOW.
WHY... I DON'T KNOW
OK I Don't ~~know~~

SORRY I KNOW YOU DONT WANT TO HEAR THAT.

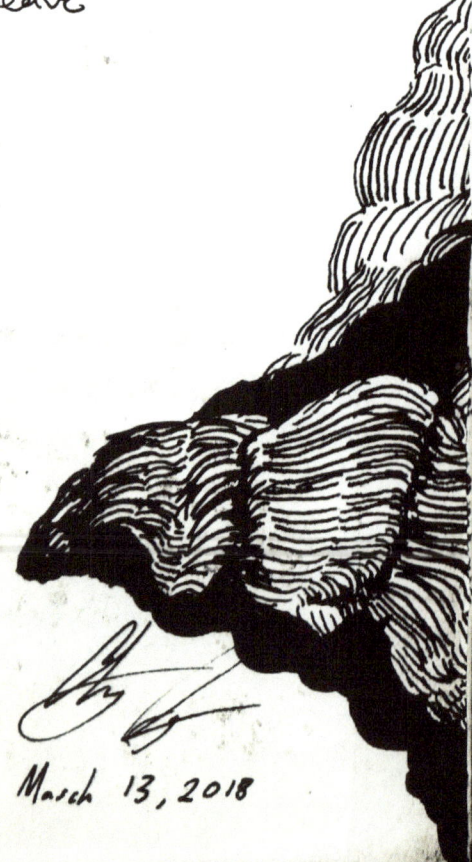

March 13, 2018

Test #1

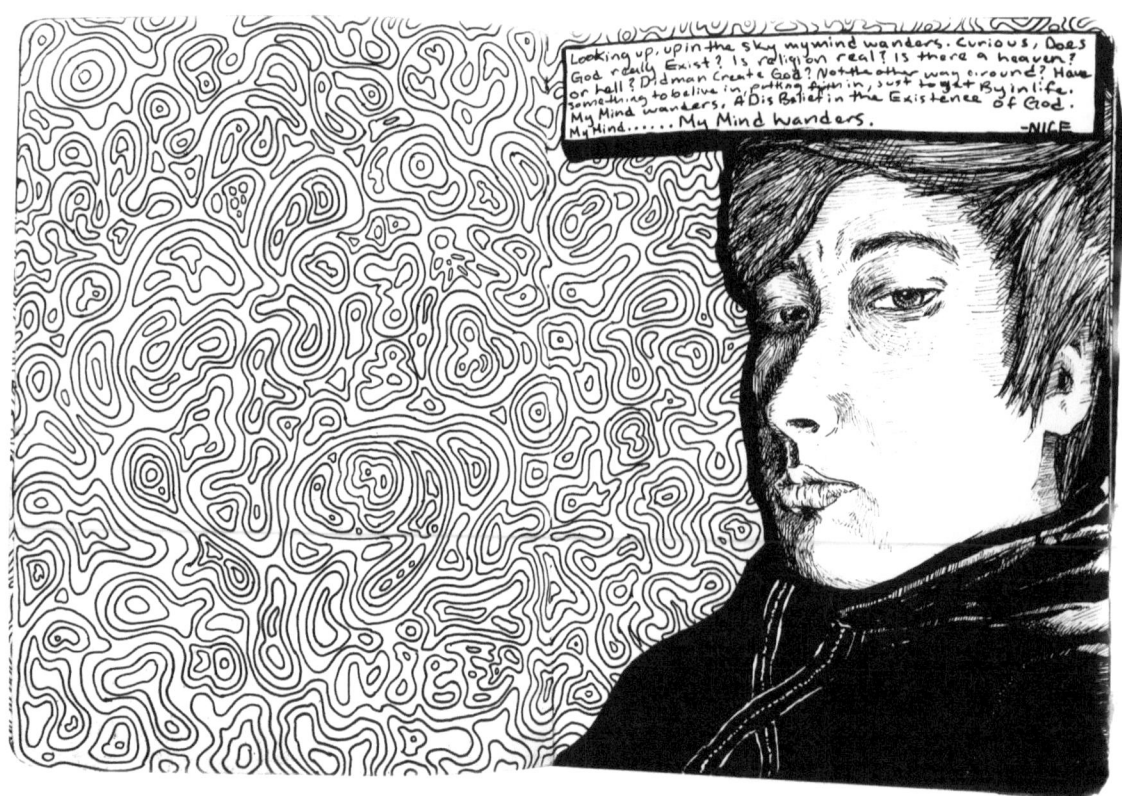

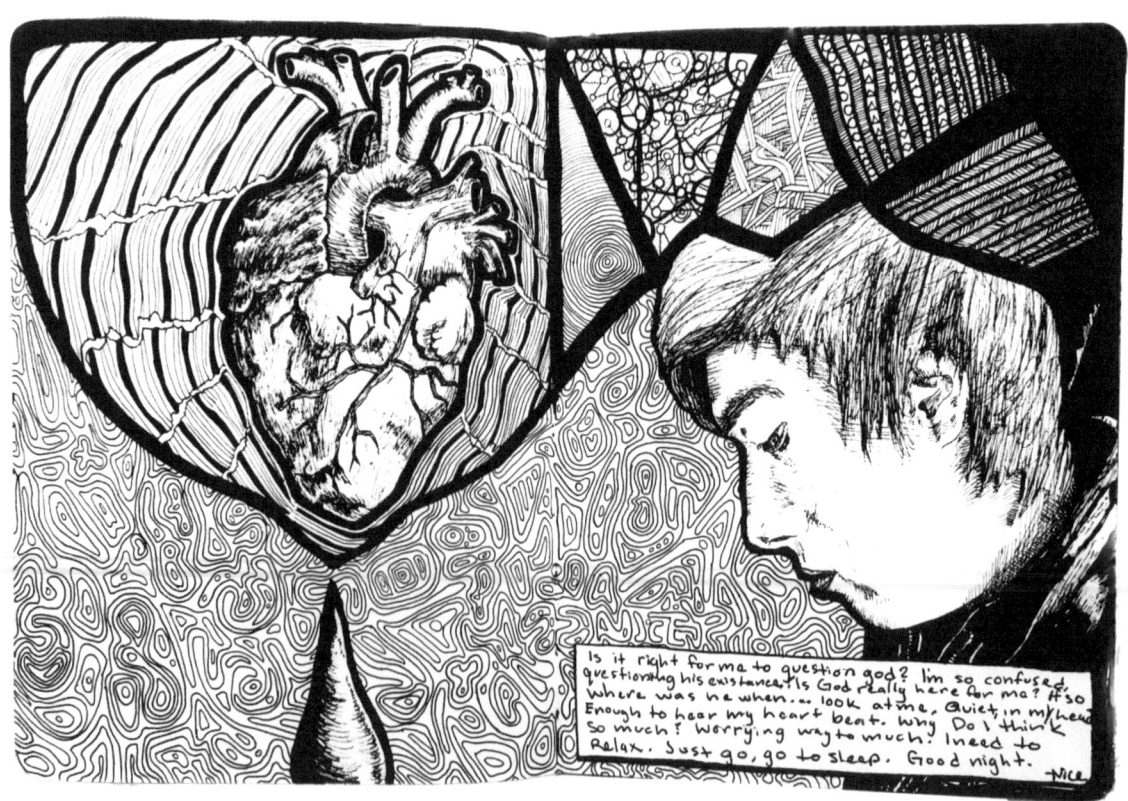

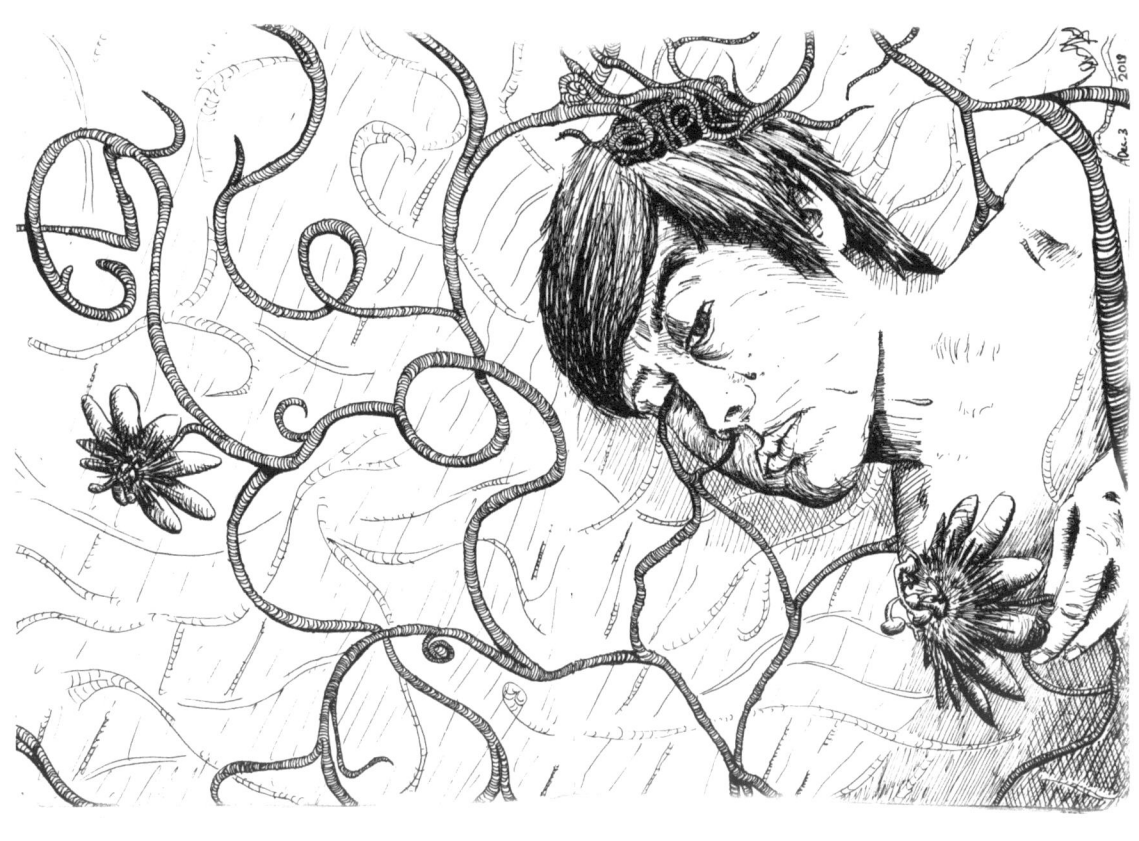
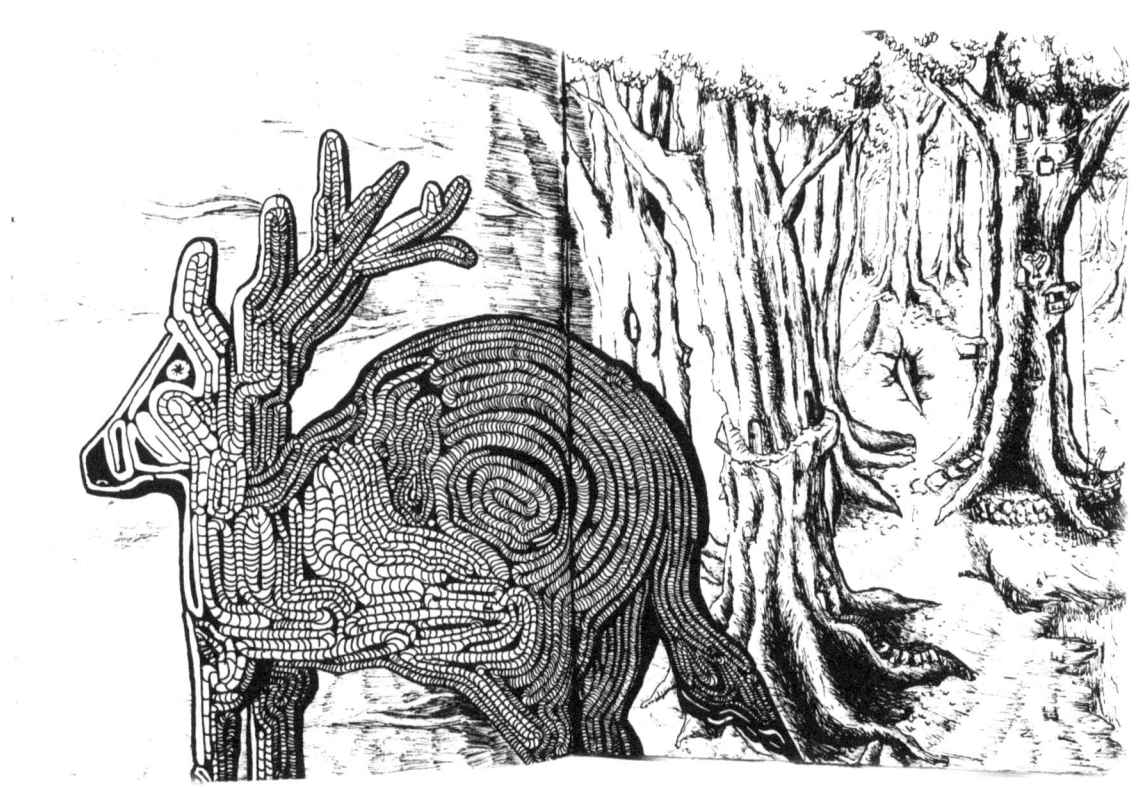

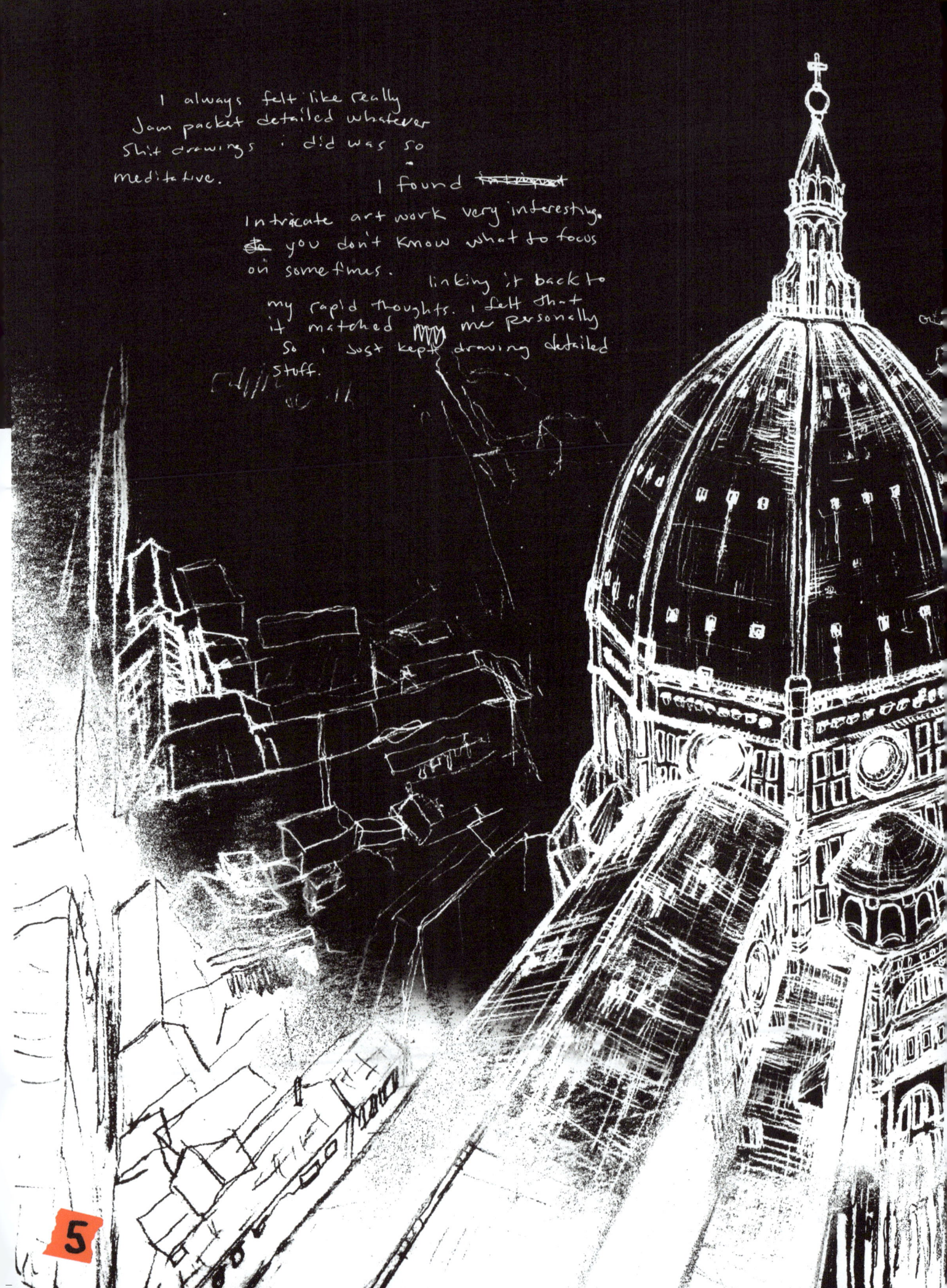

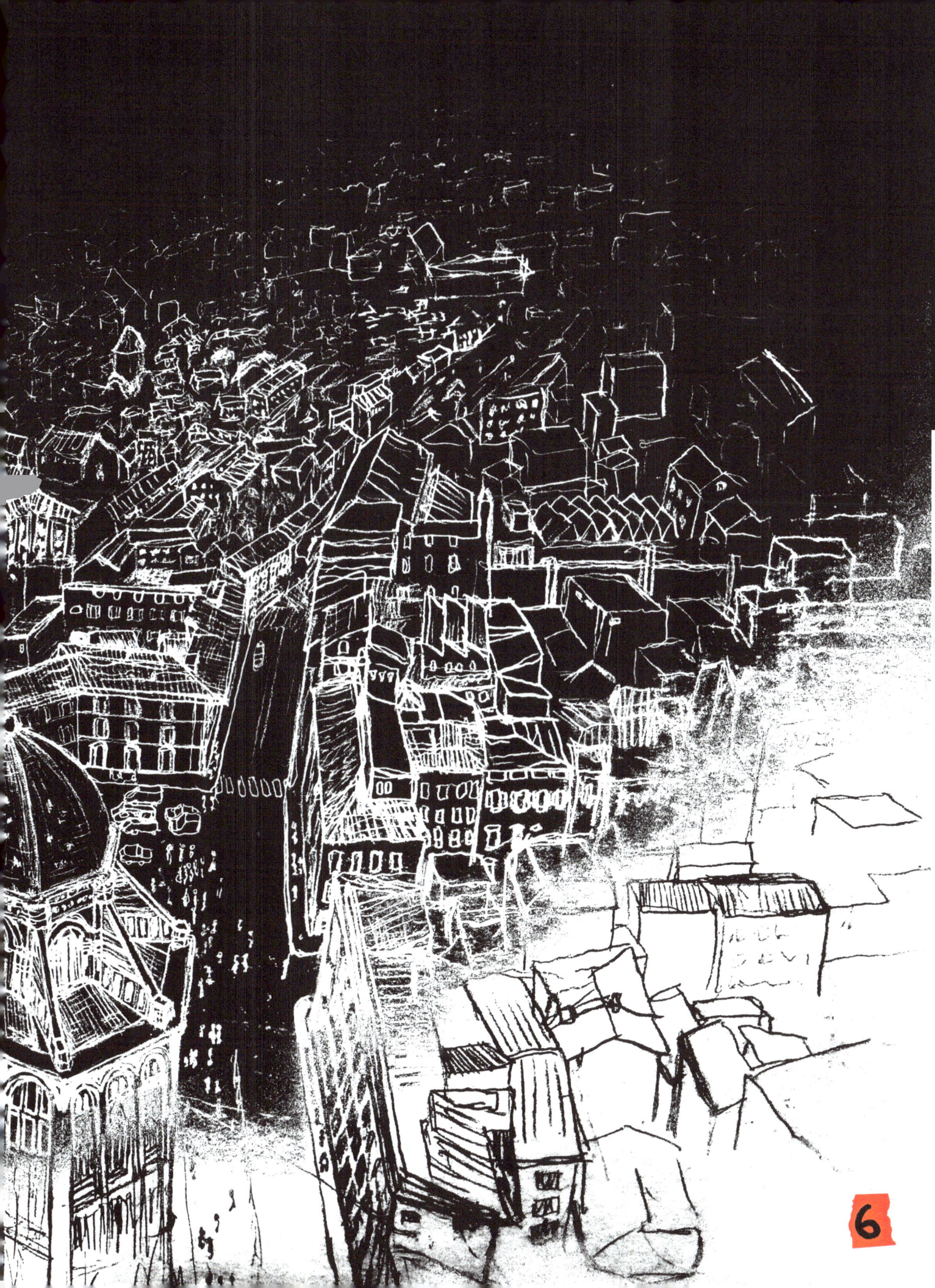

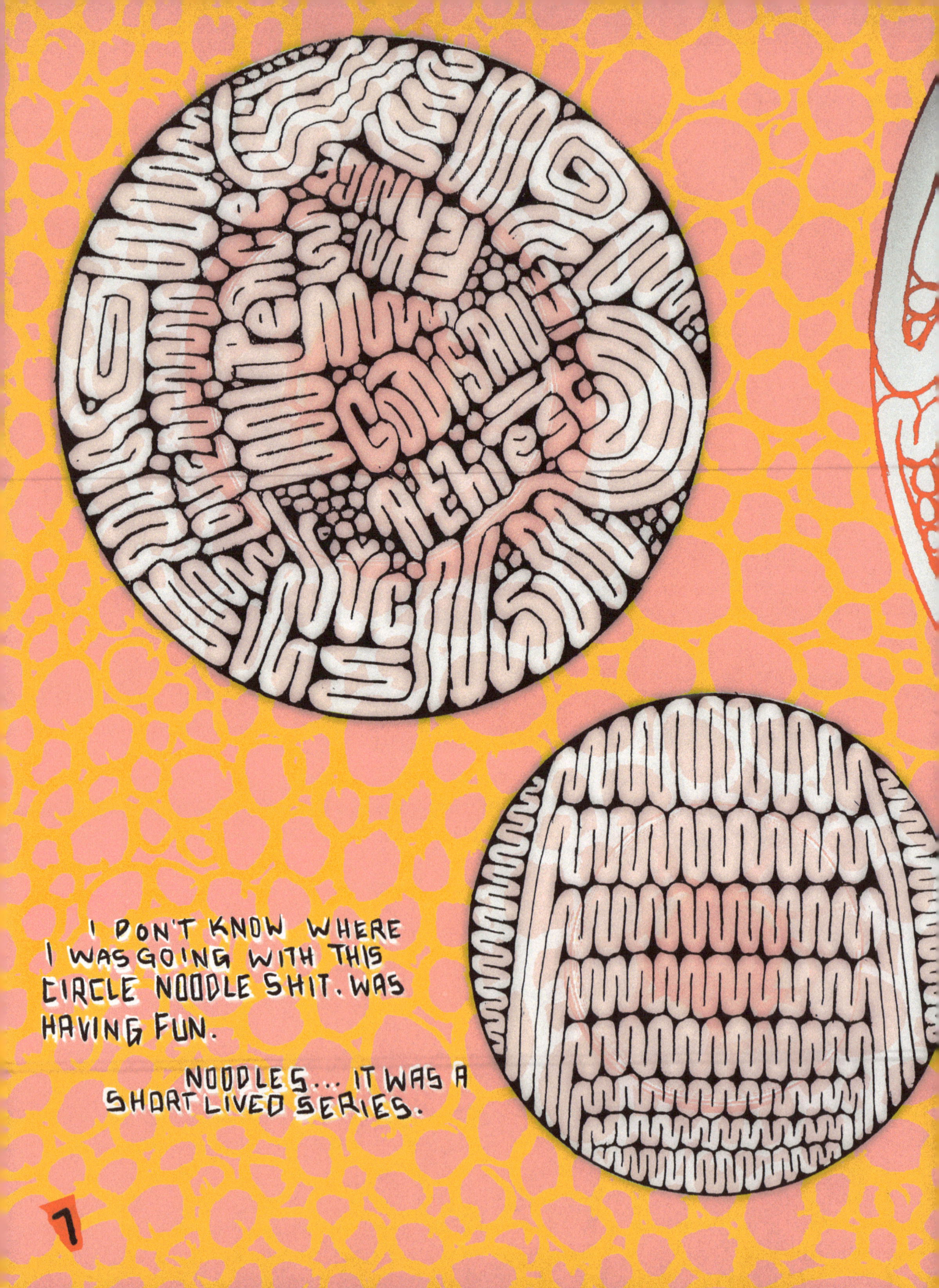

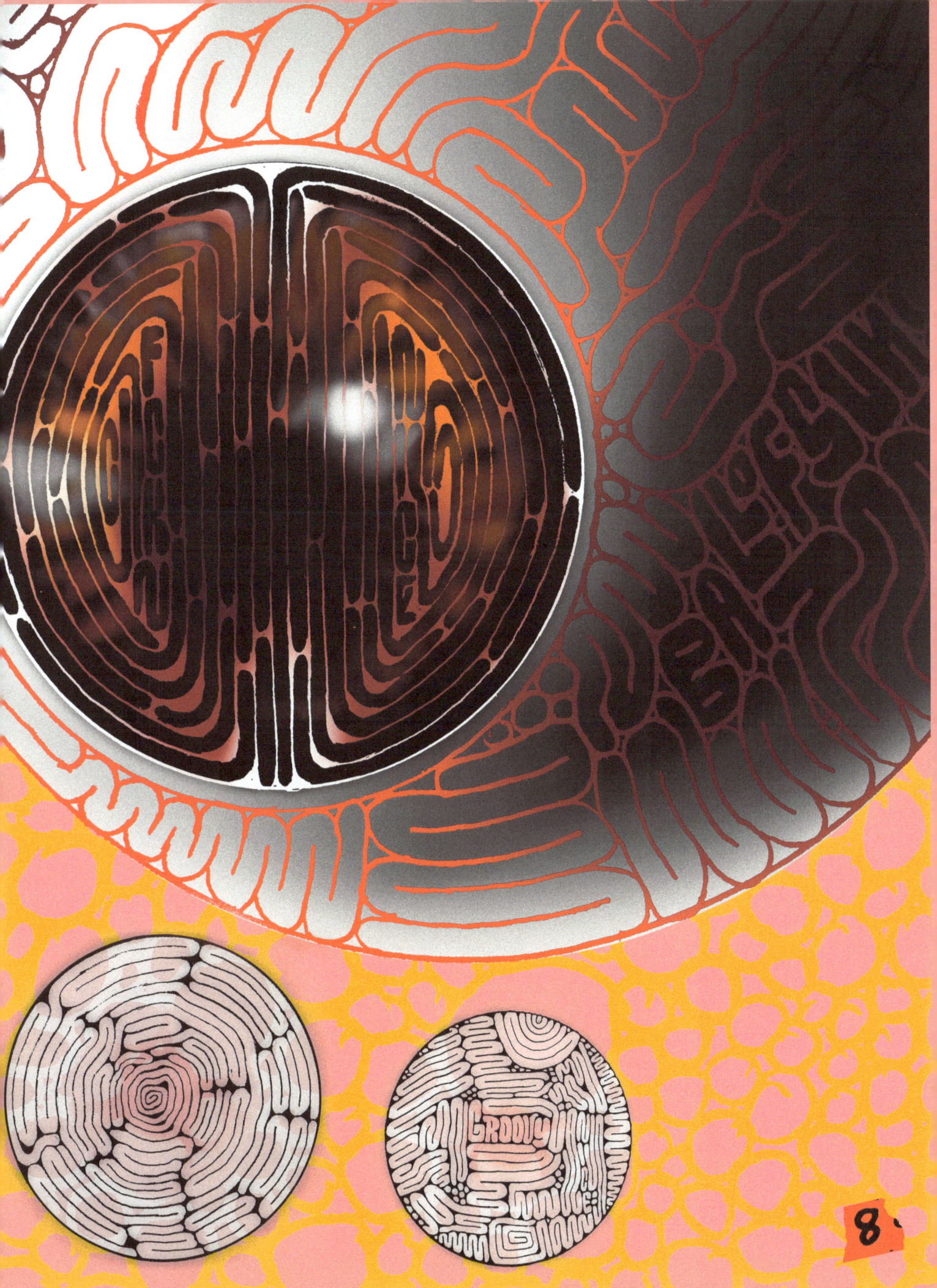

LETS MOVE TO THE NEXT PART OF THE BOOK...

I WILL SHOWCASE A SERIES OF LIQUOR STORES. THE FIRST 5 PIECES ARE THE SAME PLACE HE TOOK FOTOS OF AND THE LAST IS A REPRESENTATION OF THE "CONVENIENT" NATURE OF BEING ABLE TO FIND A LIQUOR STORE PRETTY MUCH ANYWHERE...

ALRIGHT, GO ON THEN.
FLIP THE PAGE

U R 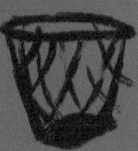 PUSSY

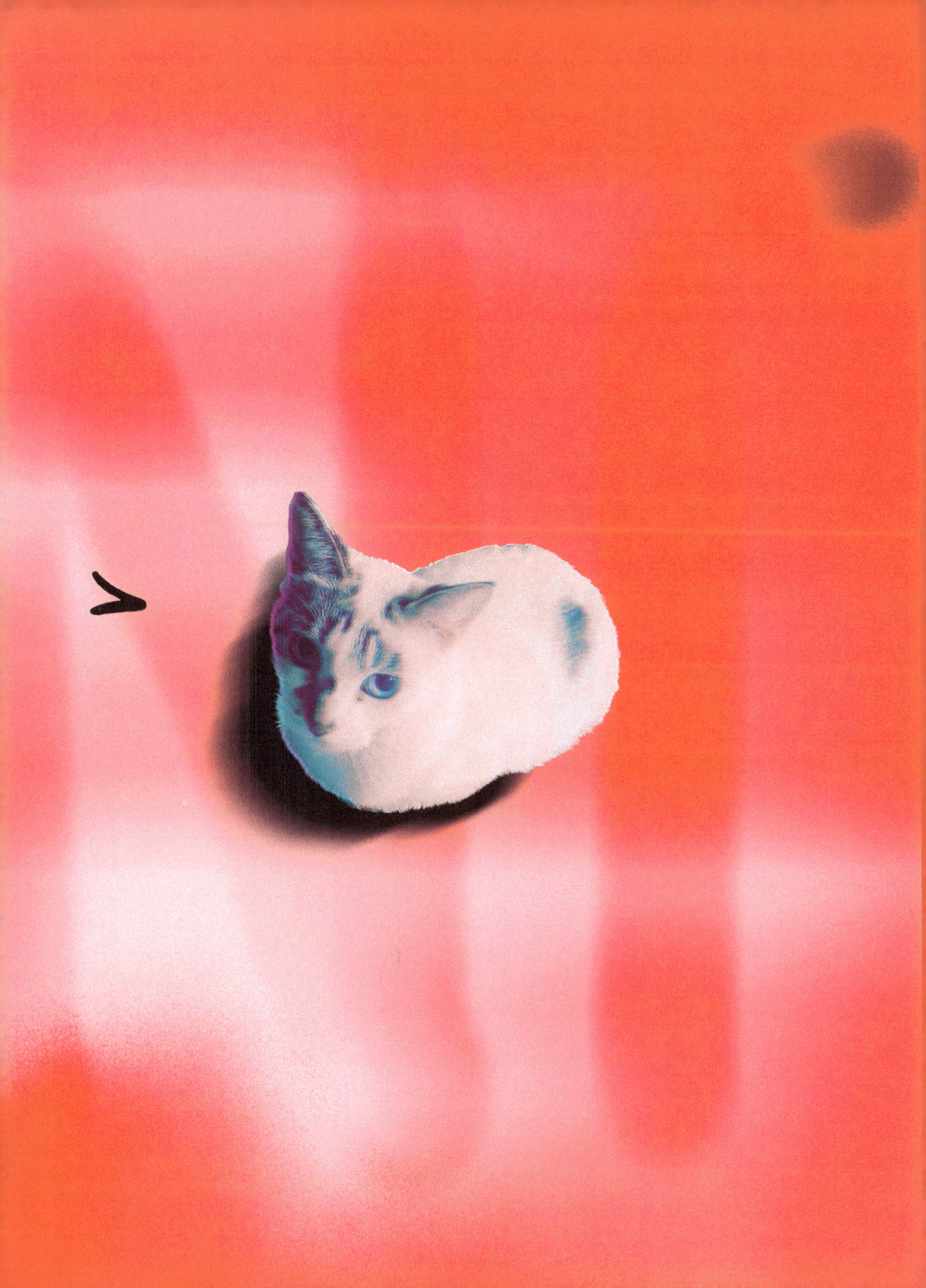

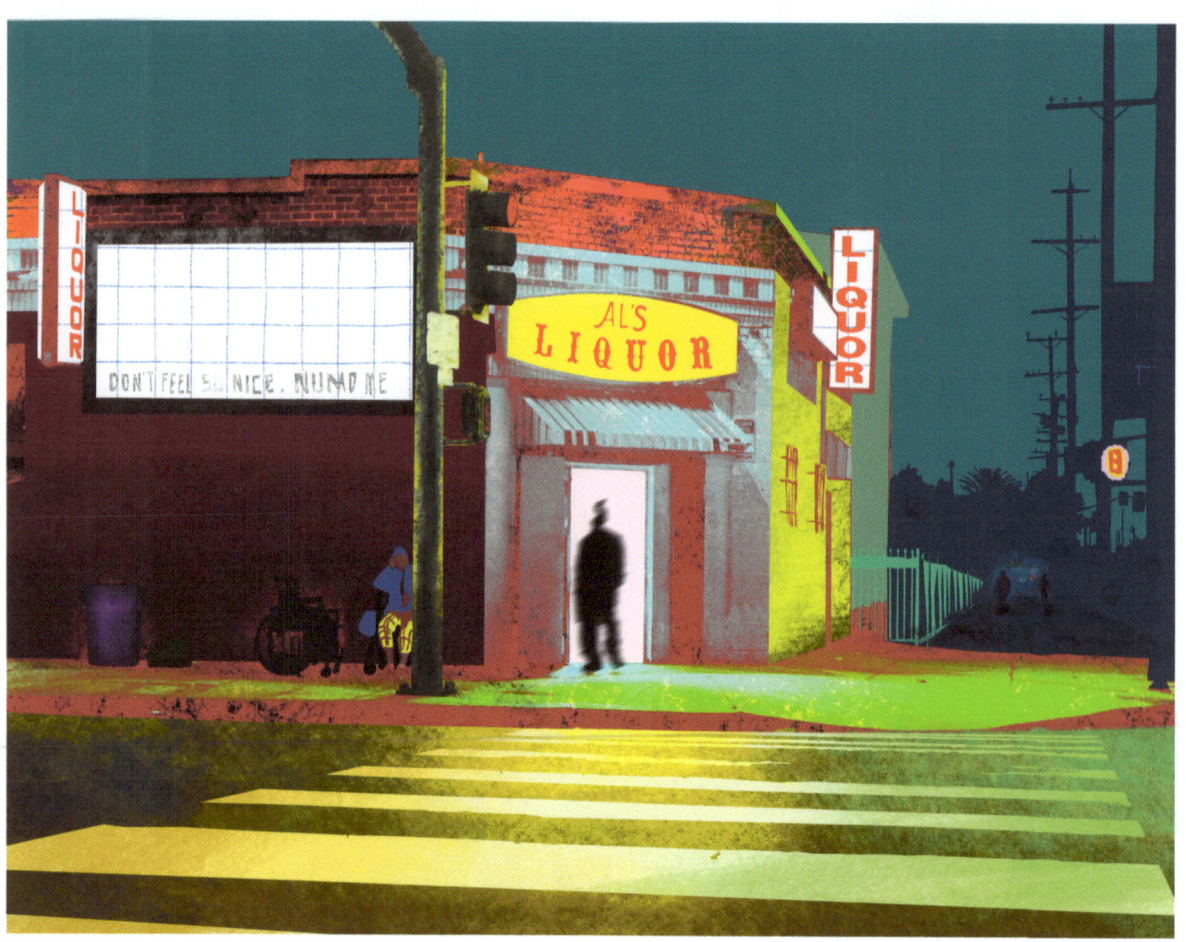
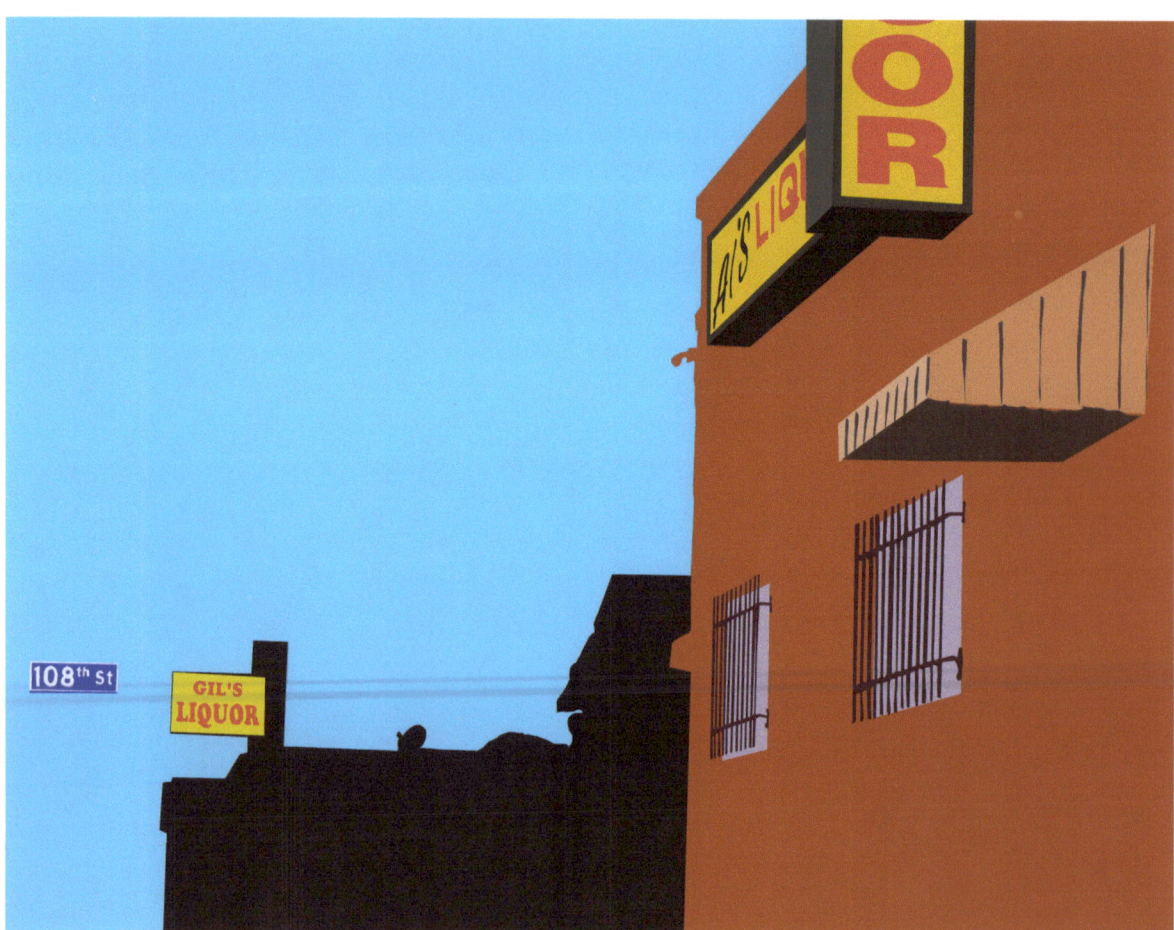

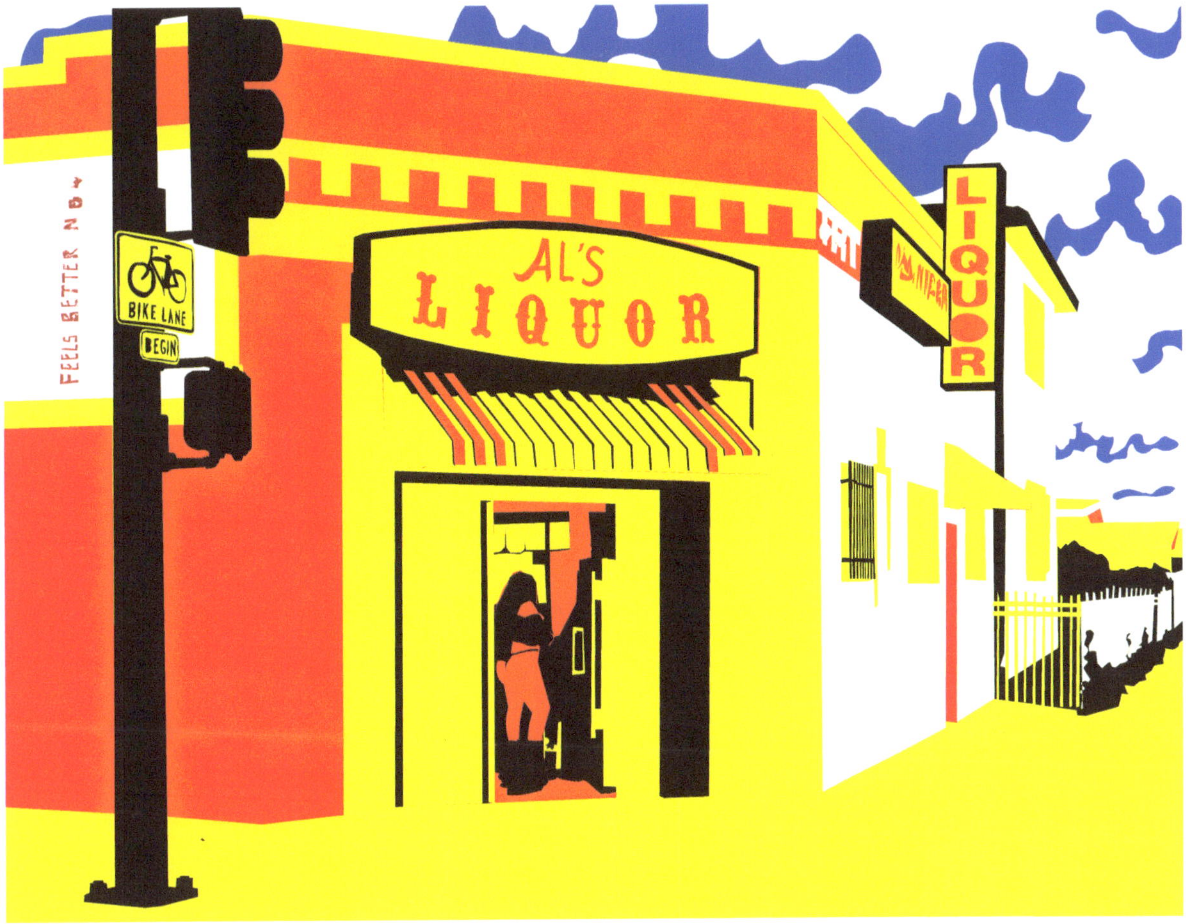

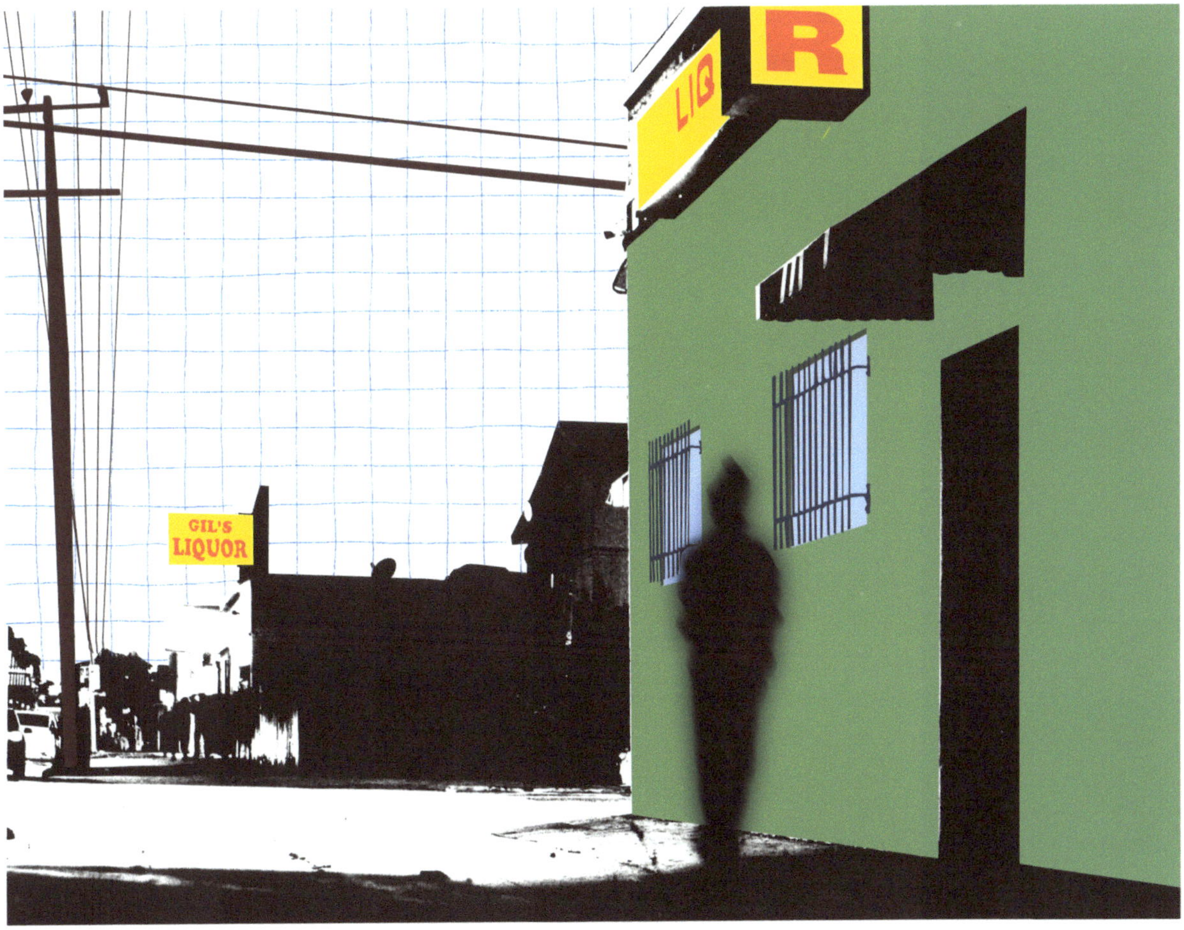

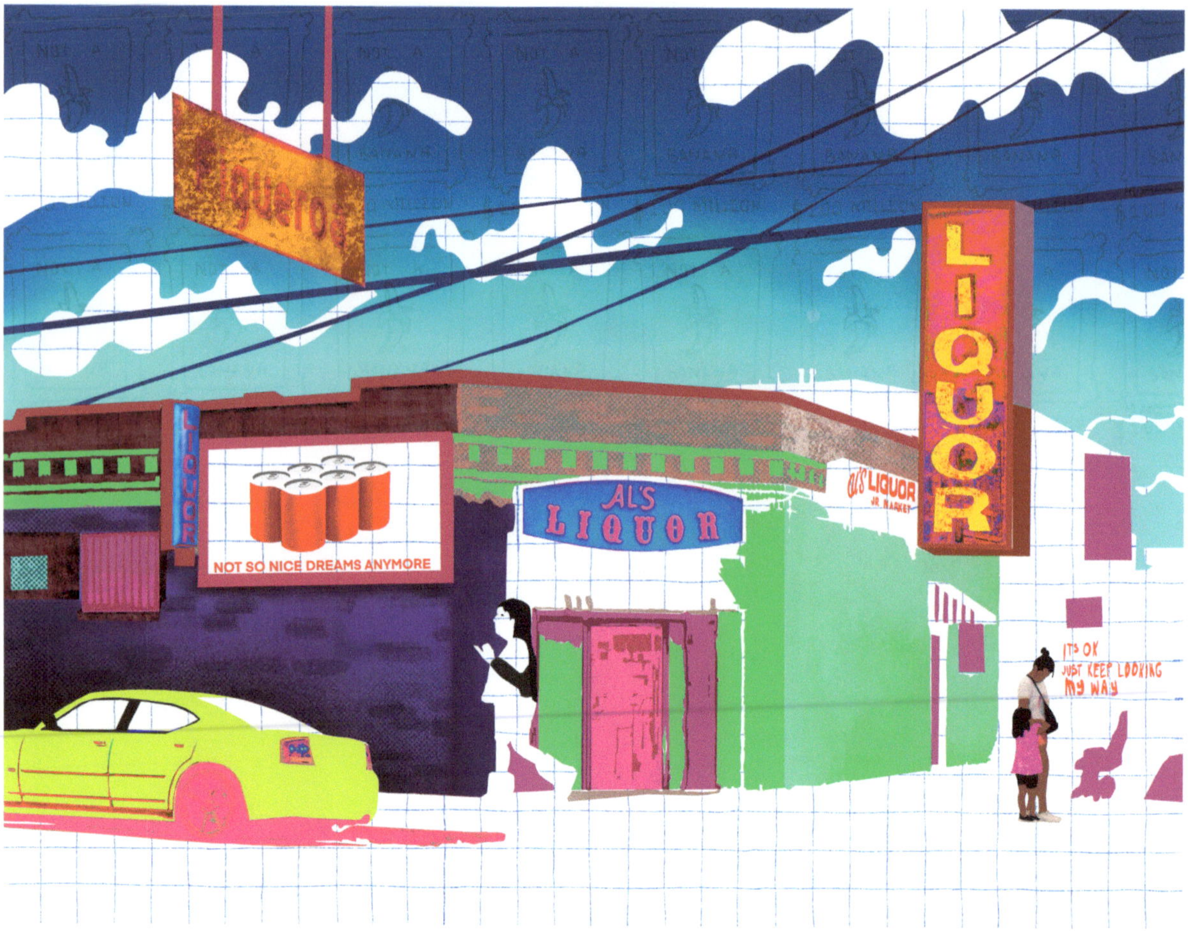

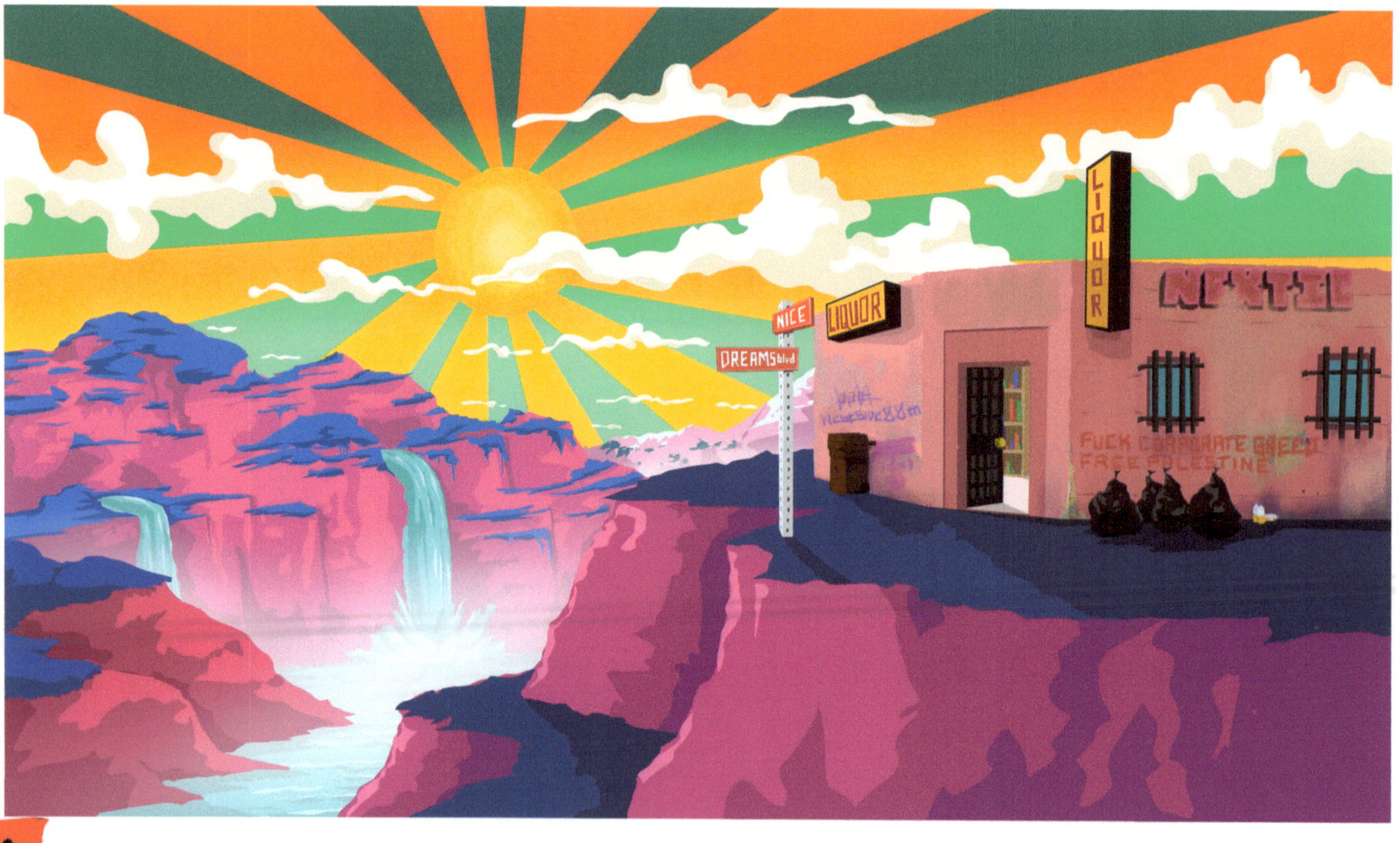

JEAN-MICHEL BASQUIRT

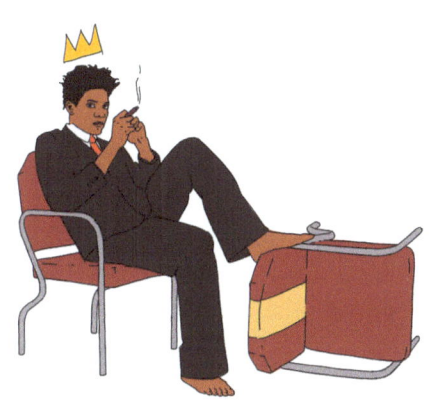

A HUGE INSPORATION OF MINE
I JUST WANTED TO MENTION THAT.
OK THATS IT...

— NICE

THIS ONE WAS FUN TO MAKE BECAUSE I INCORPORATED WHAT I LEARNED DIGITALLY ~ AND ADDED MY TRADITIONAL LINE NOW

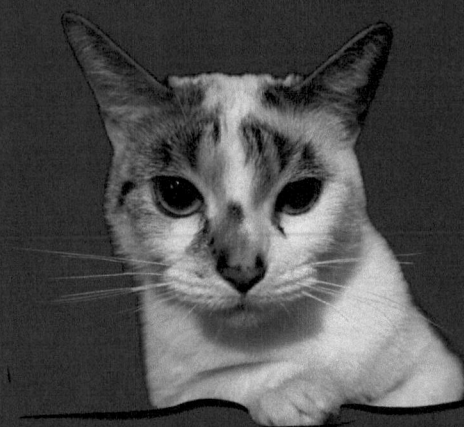

AYY!! AYY!! I'M THE NARRATOR!

DON'T BE TOUCHING MY FAVORITE PEN BITCH BOY.

ALSO YOU LIKE USING THE WORD PUSSY TOO MUCH ITS OFENSIVE TO MY KIND

ANYWAYS... AS FOR YOU.. GO TO THE NEXT PAGE

PUSSY

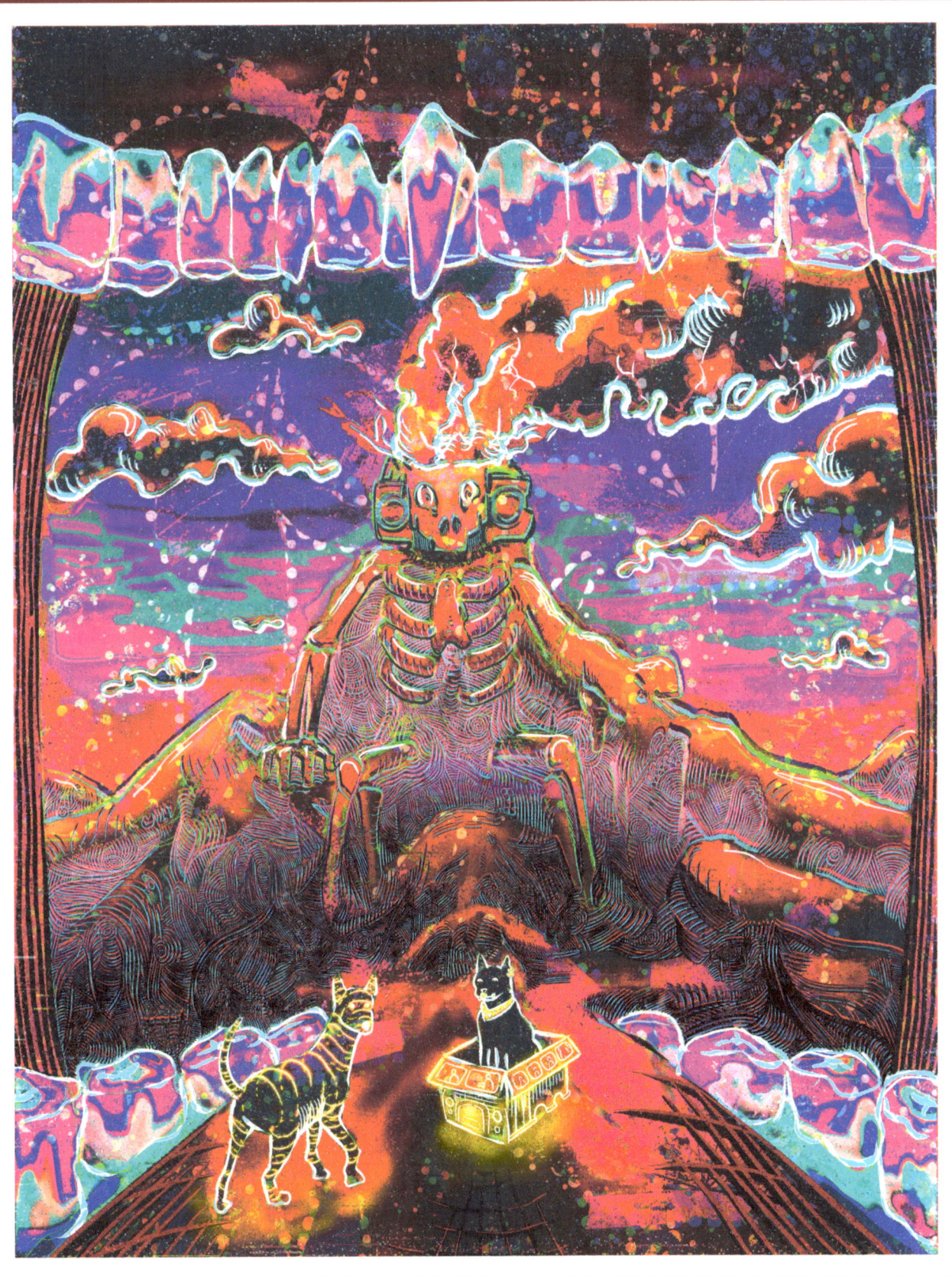

HAWKINS HOUSE OF BURGERS

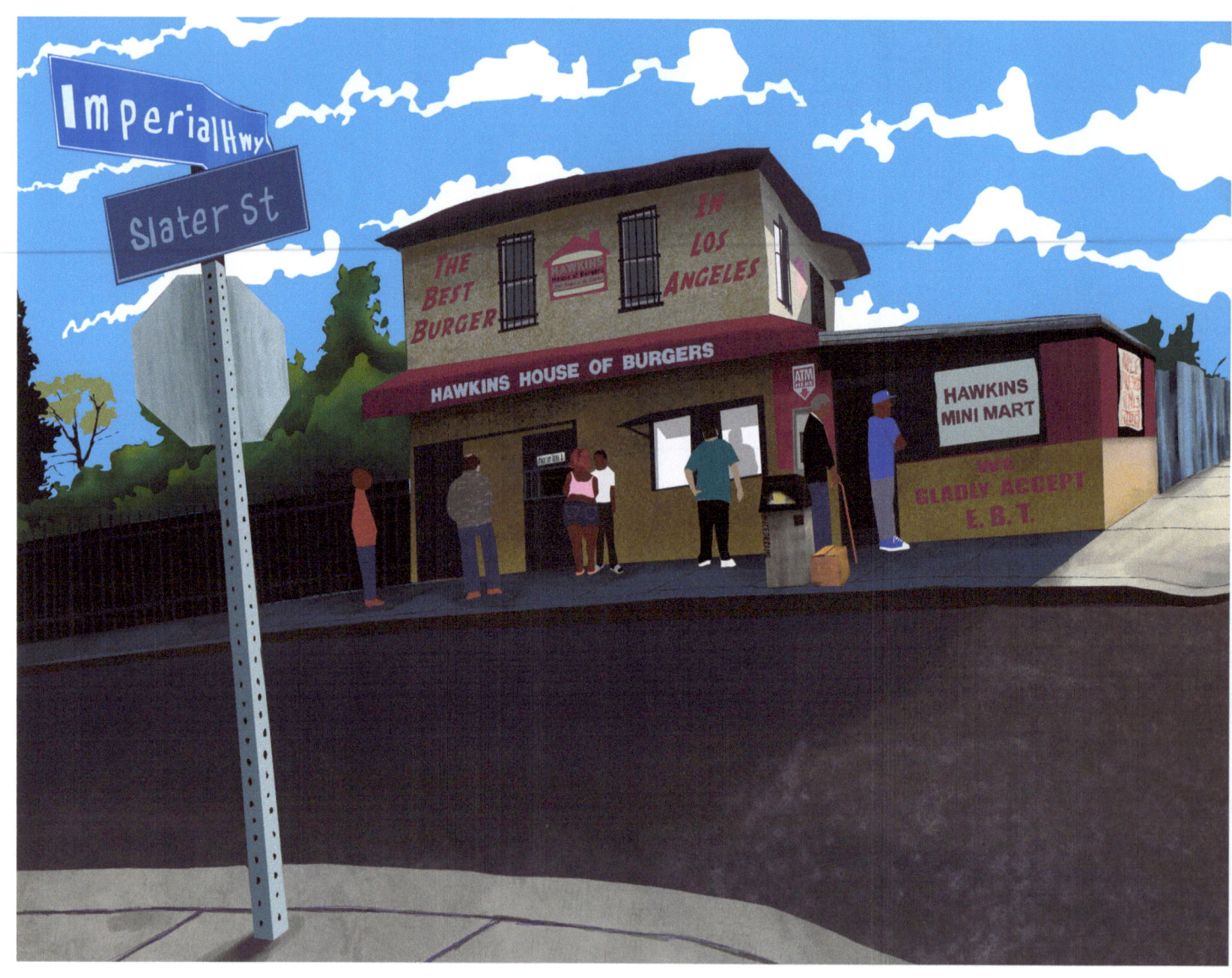

LISTEN HERE MAN...

This place got some good food. Fries are elite. On the same level as Tams fries. Then as you wait, walk over to <u>BROTHA ROOTS</u> for all things African.

Soap, all kinds of herbs for teas, sents for body and house. Cool Jude

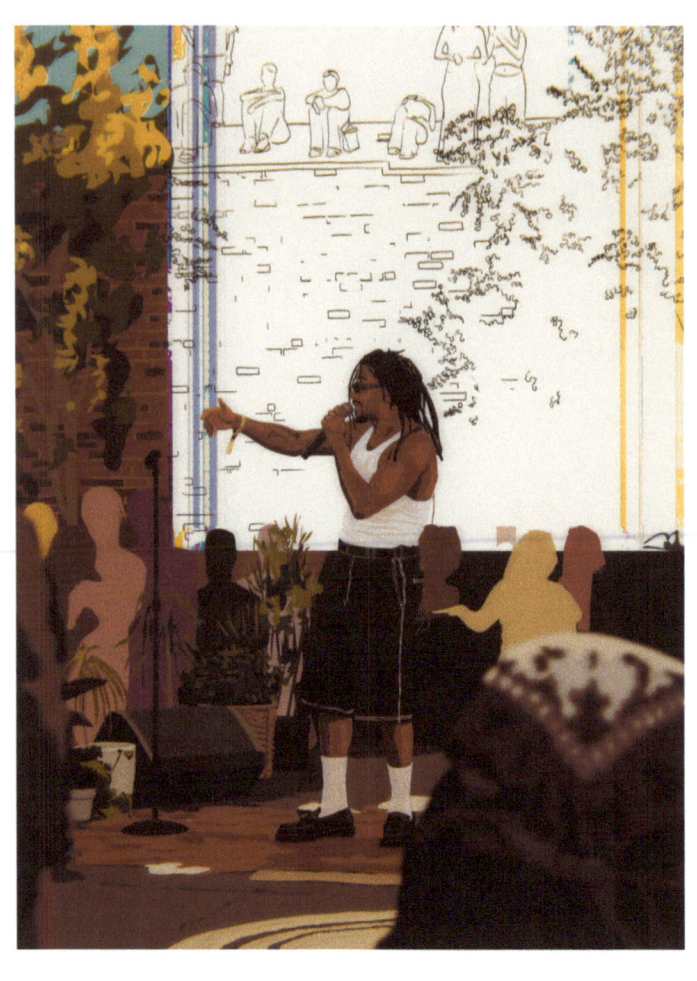

BRO JORDAN WARD WAS FUN TO WATCH PERFORM. SO I DREW THIS TO REMEMBER THE DAY. AS IT WAS.

MAN IT WOULD BE COOL TO DRAW LIKE THIS MORE. I NEVER REALLY SHOWCASE THIS STYLE OF ART.

MAYBE LATER

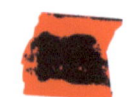

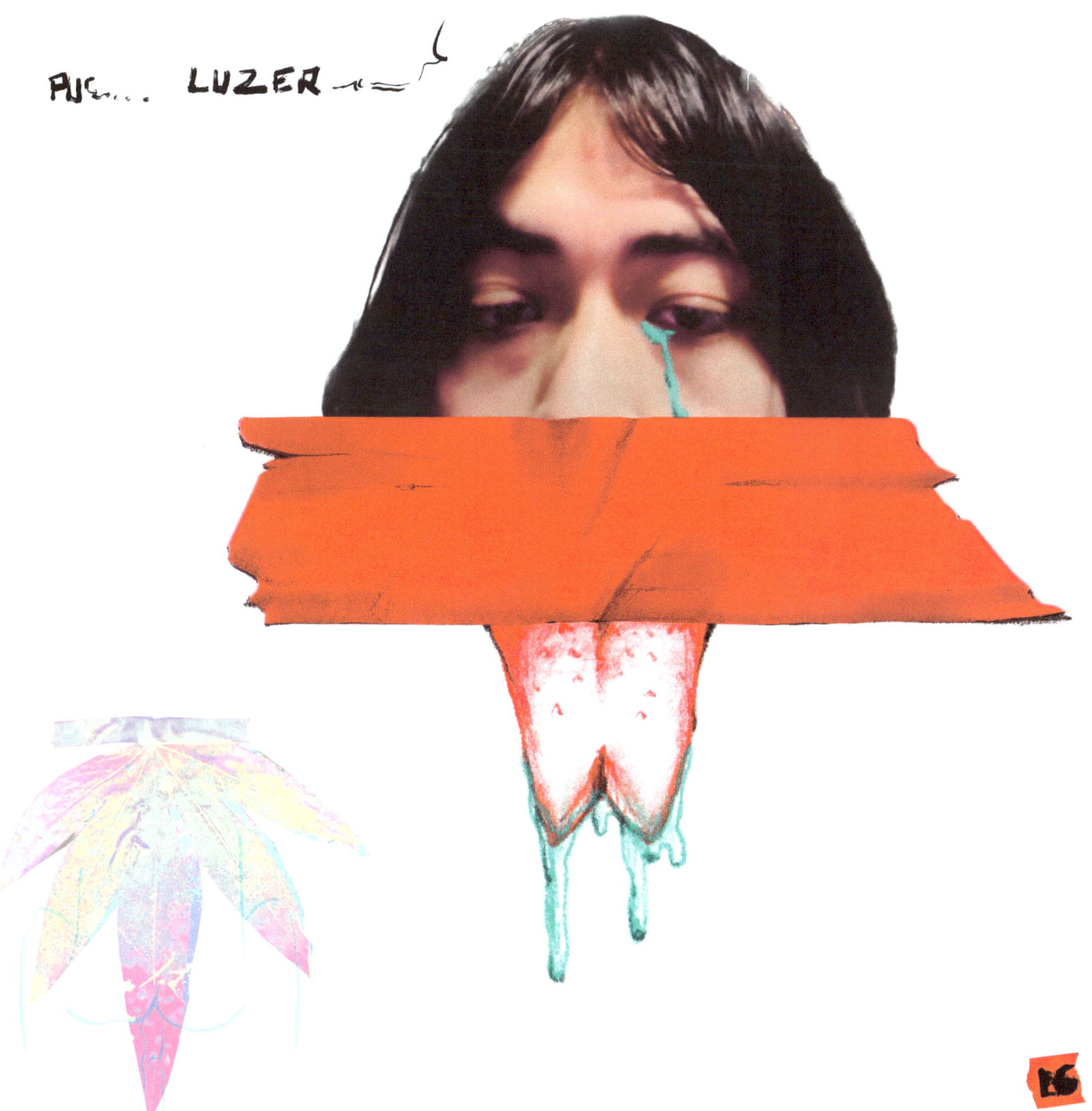

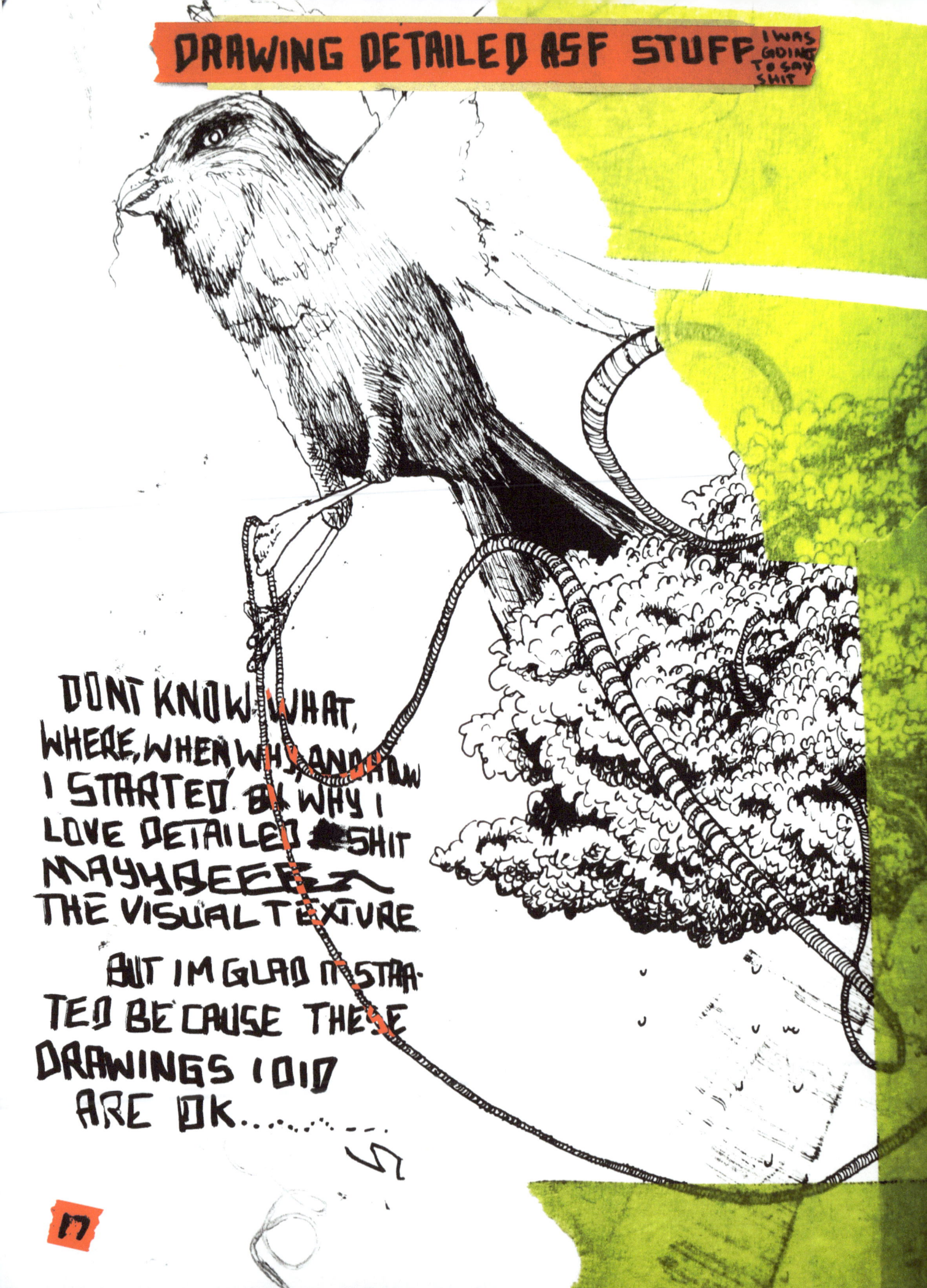

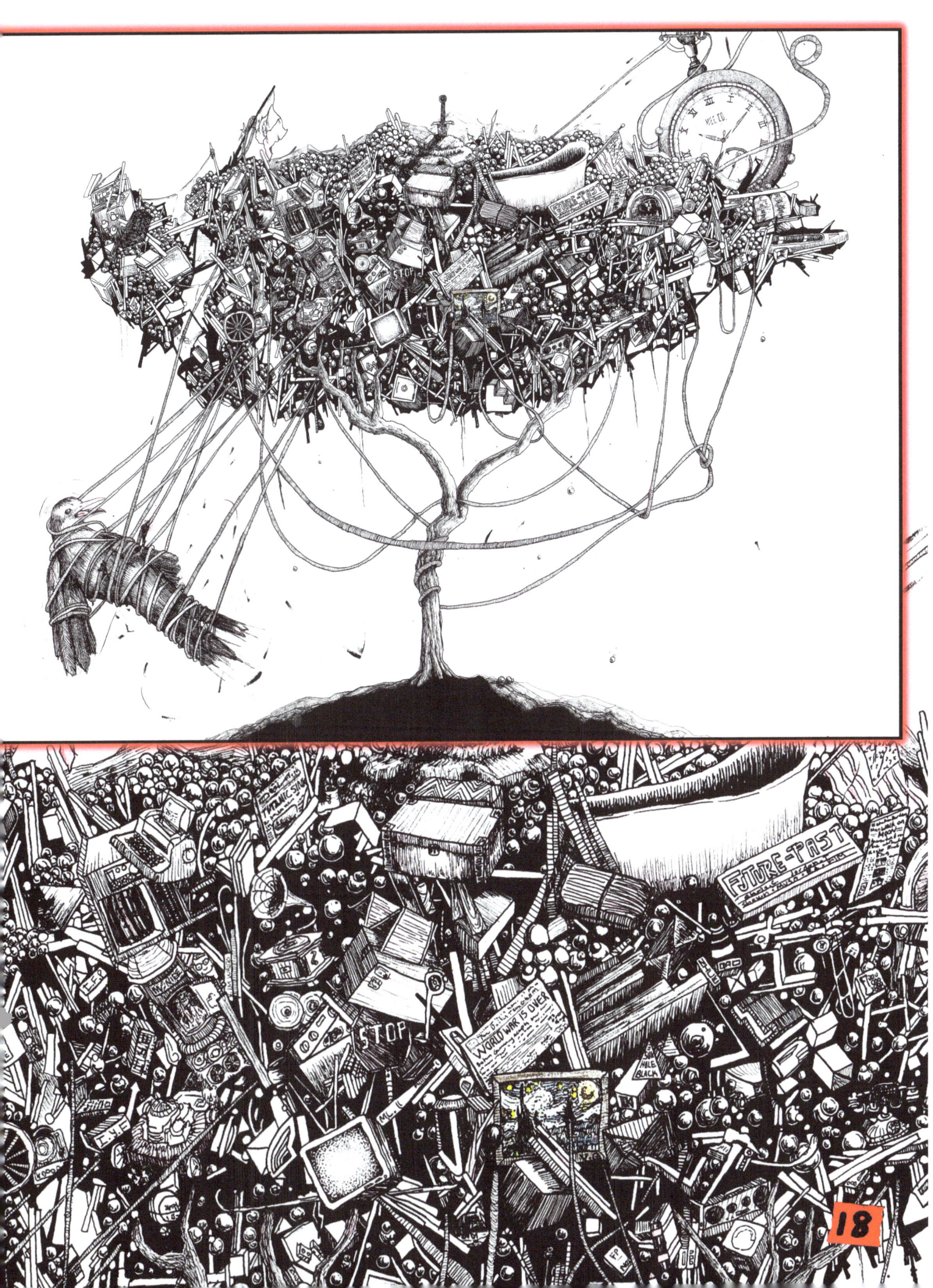

THIS DRAWING BELOW COMBINED WITH PAGE 15 WAS THE INSPIRATION FOR THE JUNK TREE. ↓

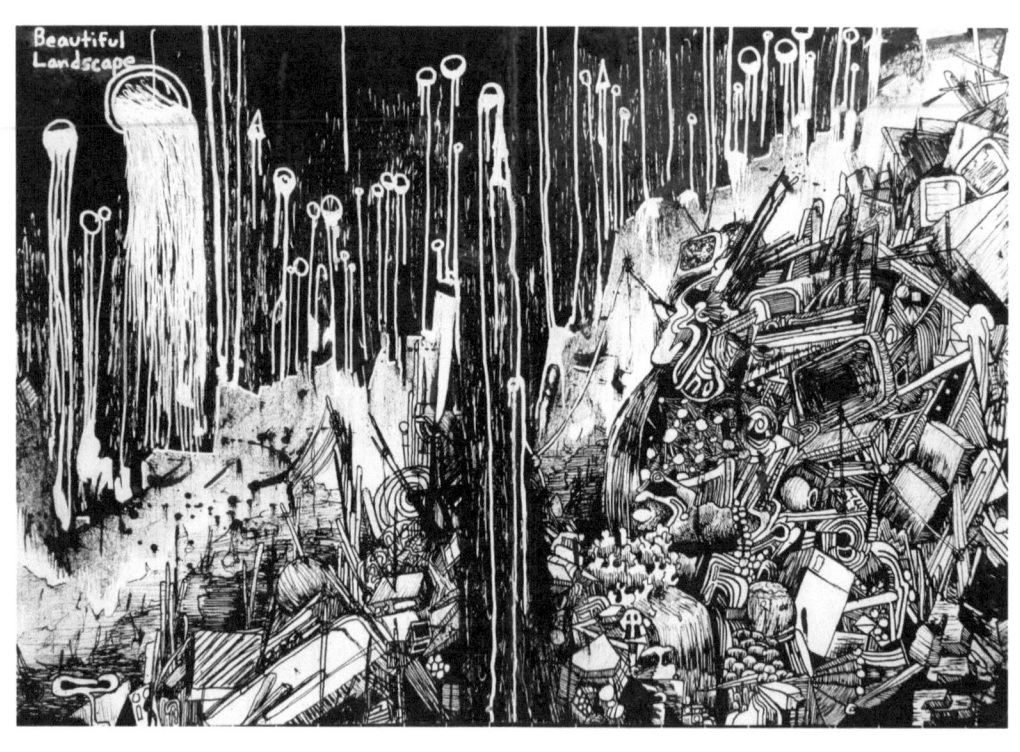

I AM SON OF DREAMS, I TEND TO HAVE NICE DREAMS ONLY.

I'M ONLY DREAMING, PLEASE STAND BY

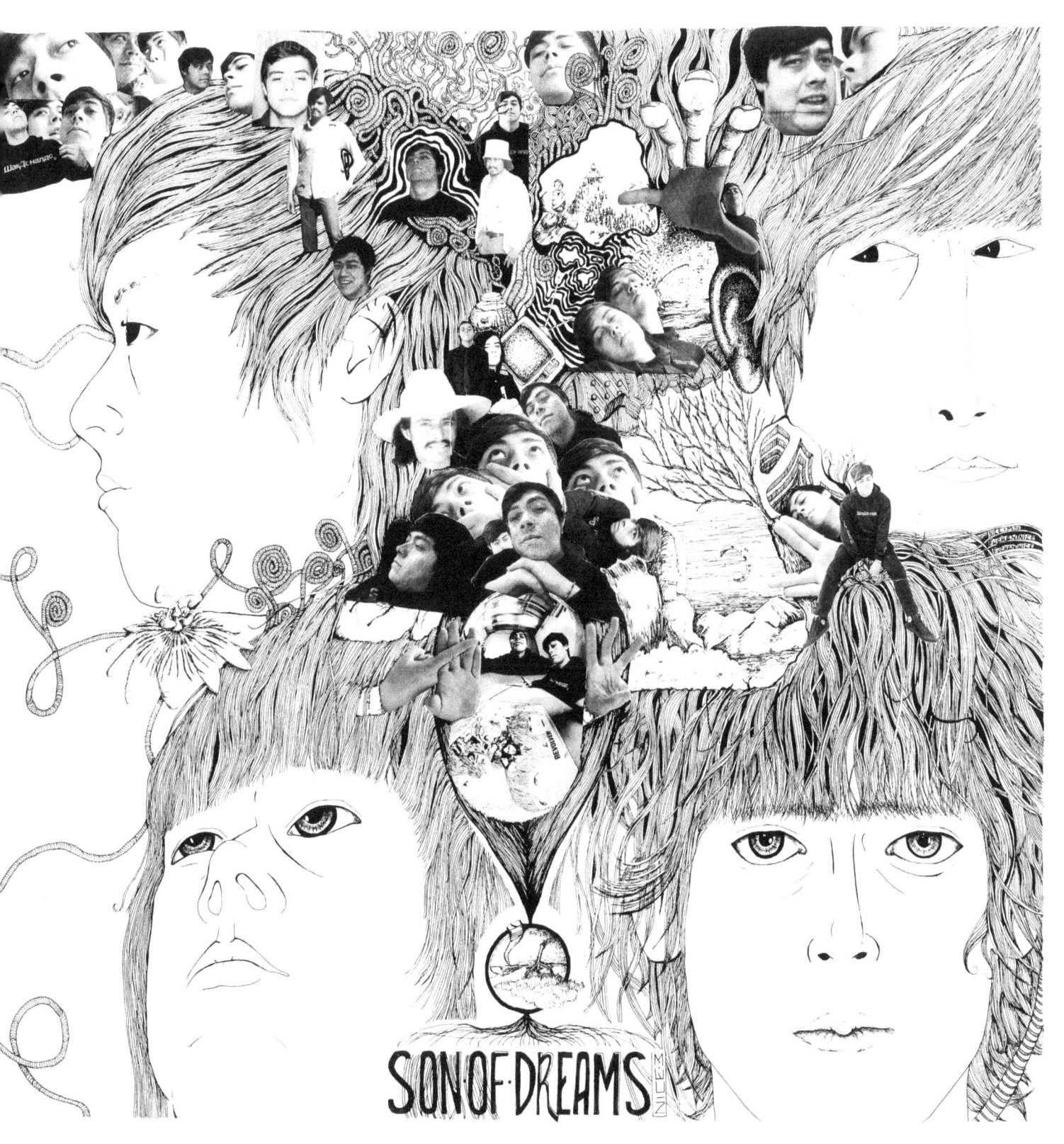

SELF PORTRAIT

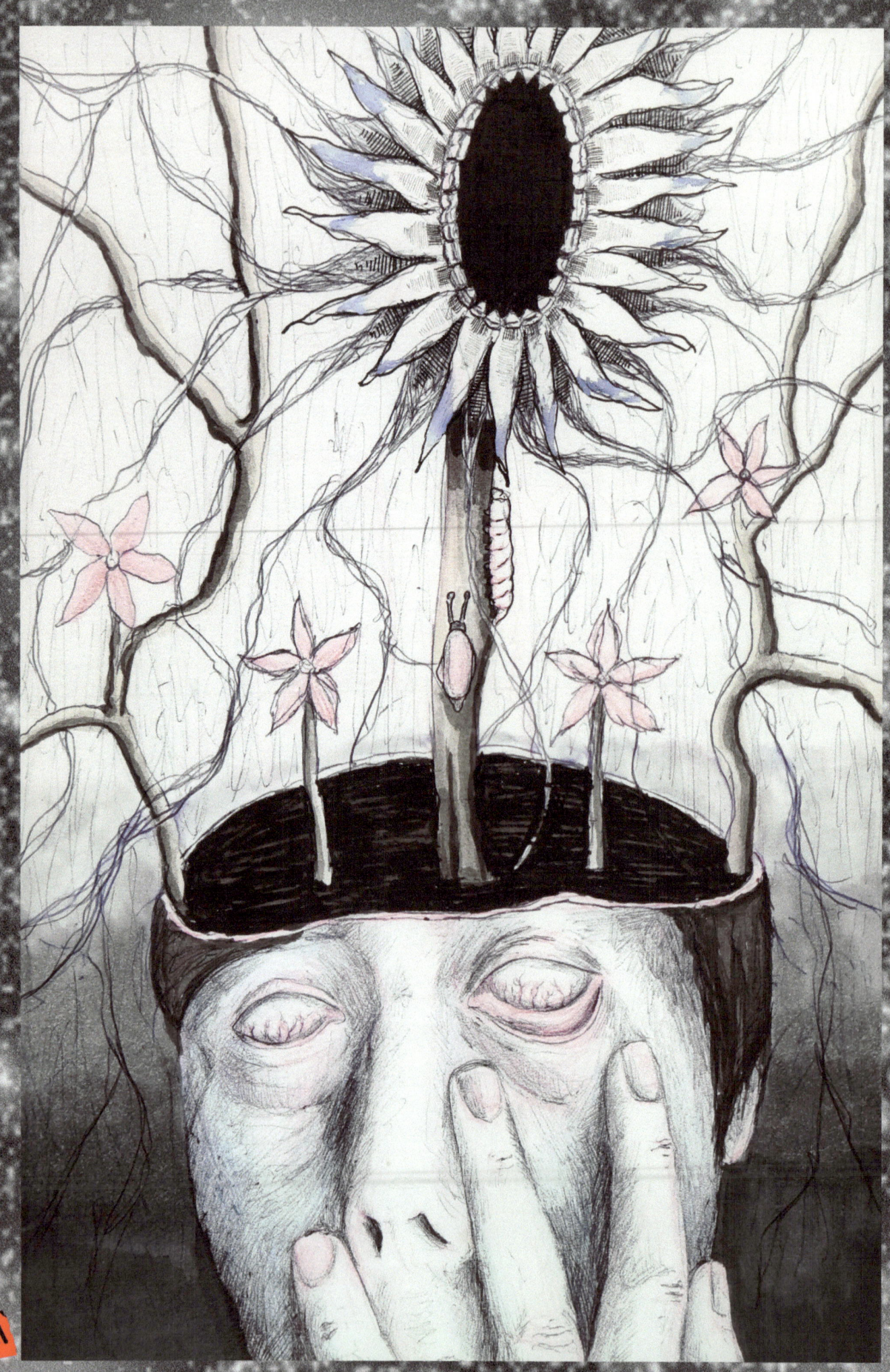

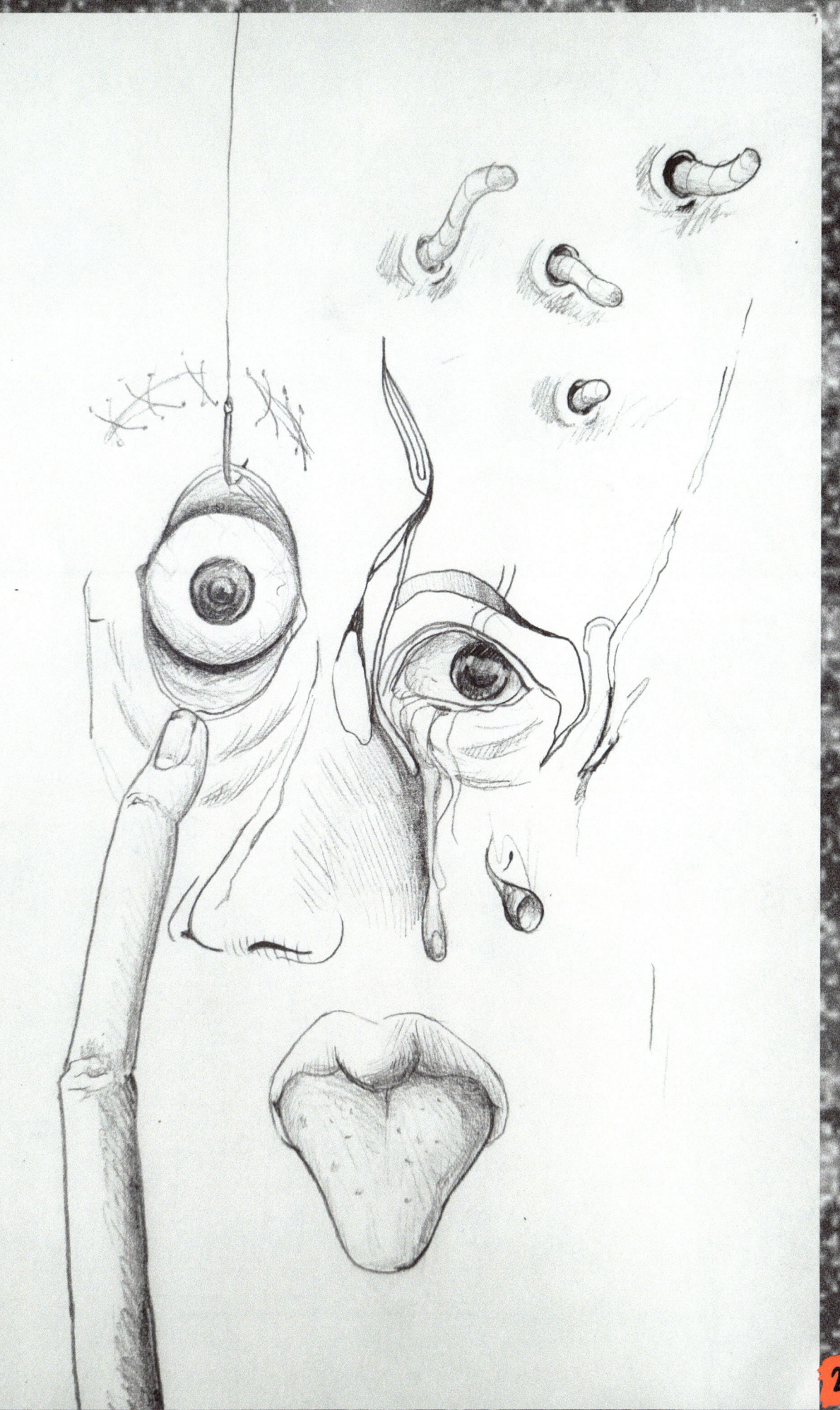

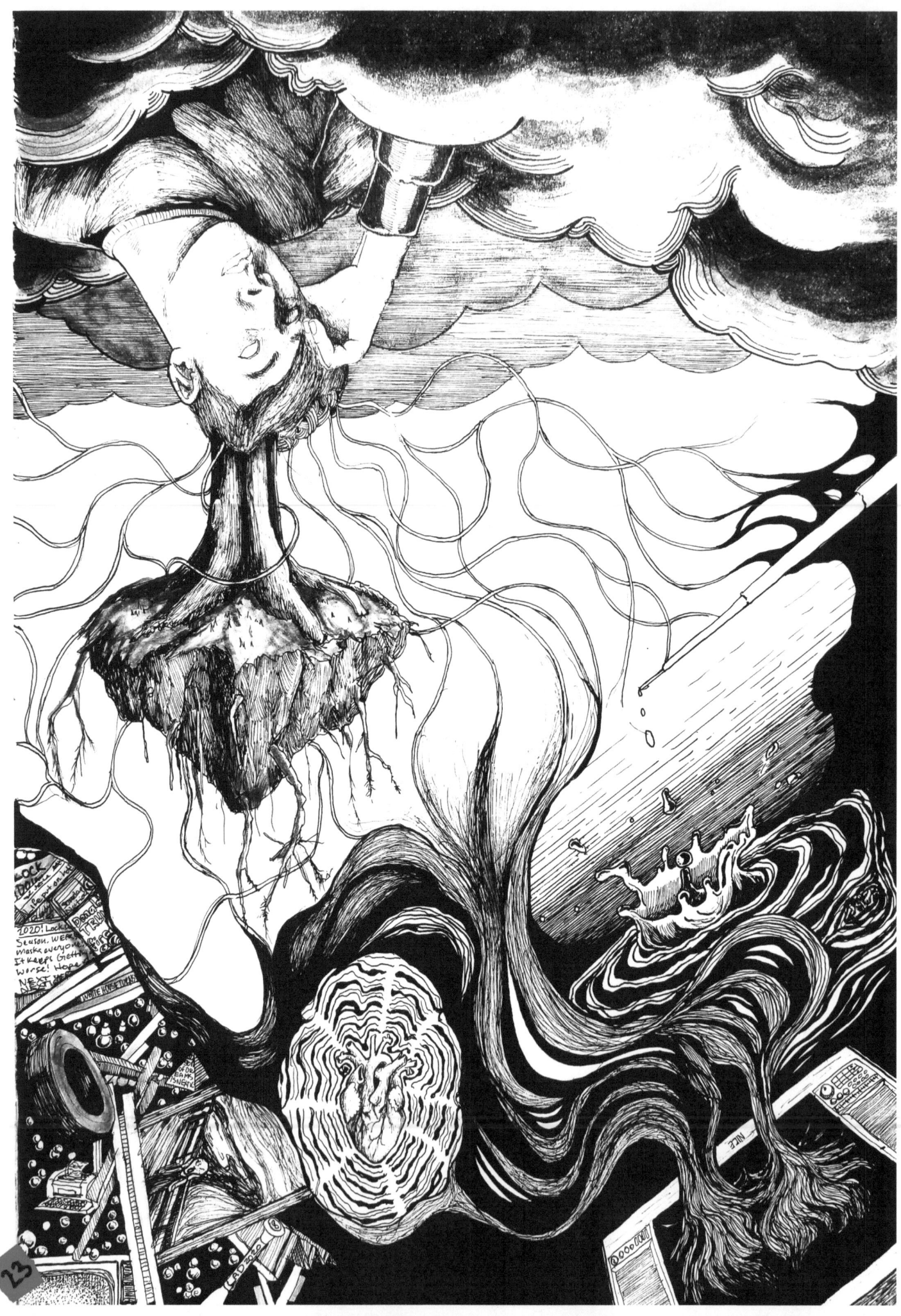

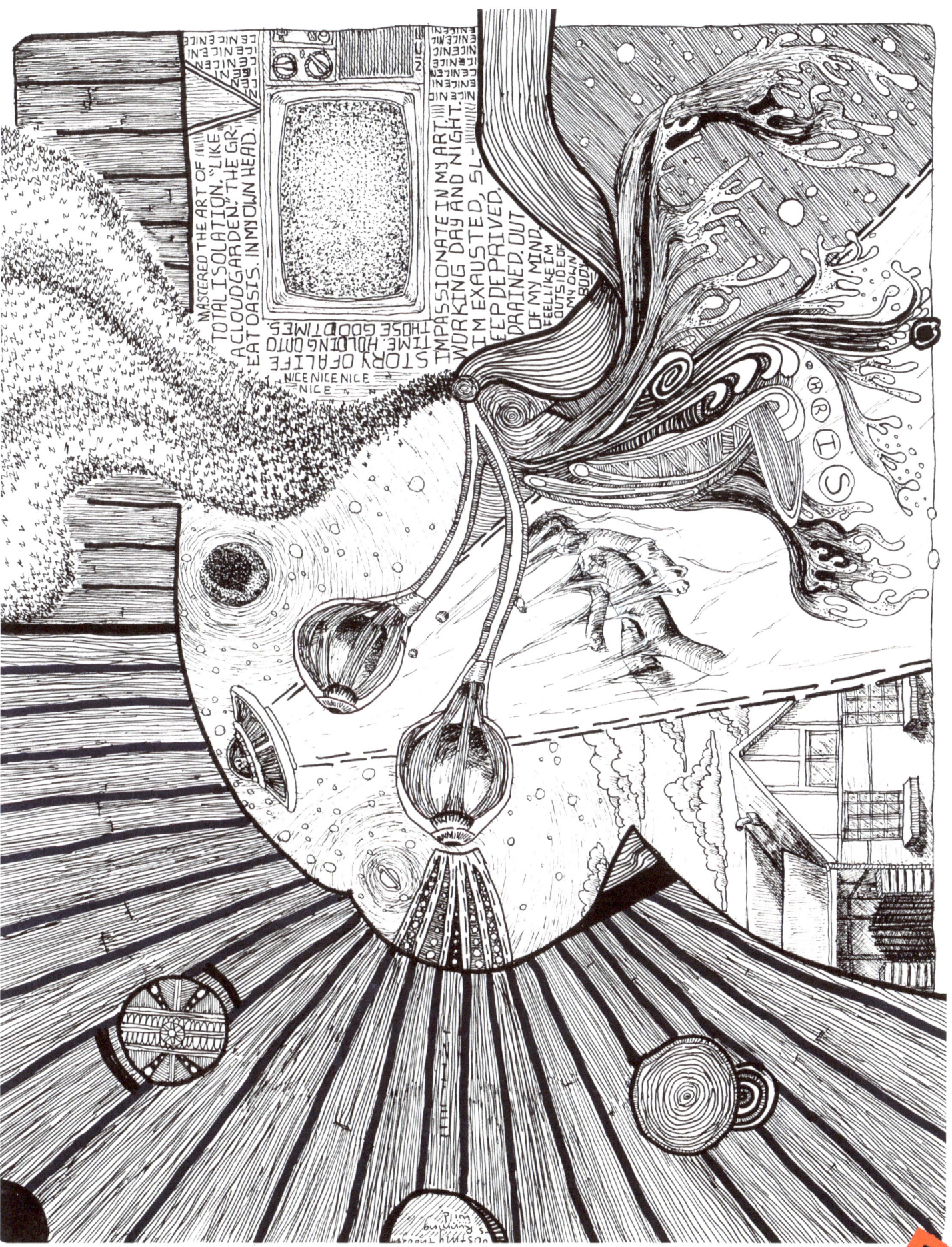

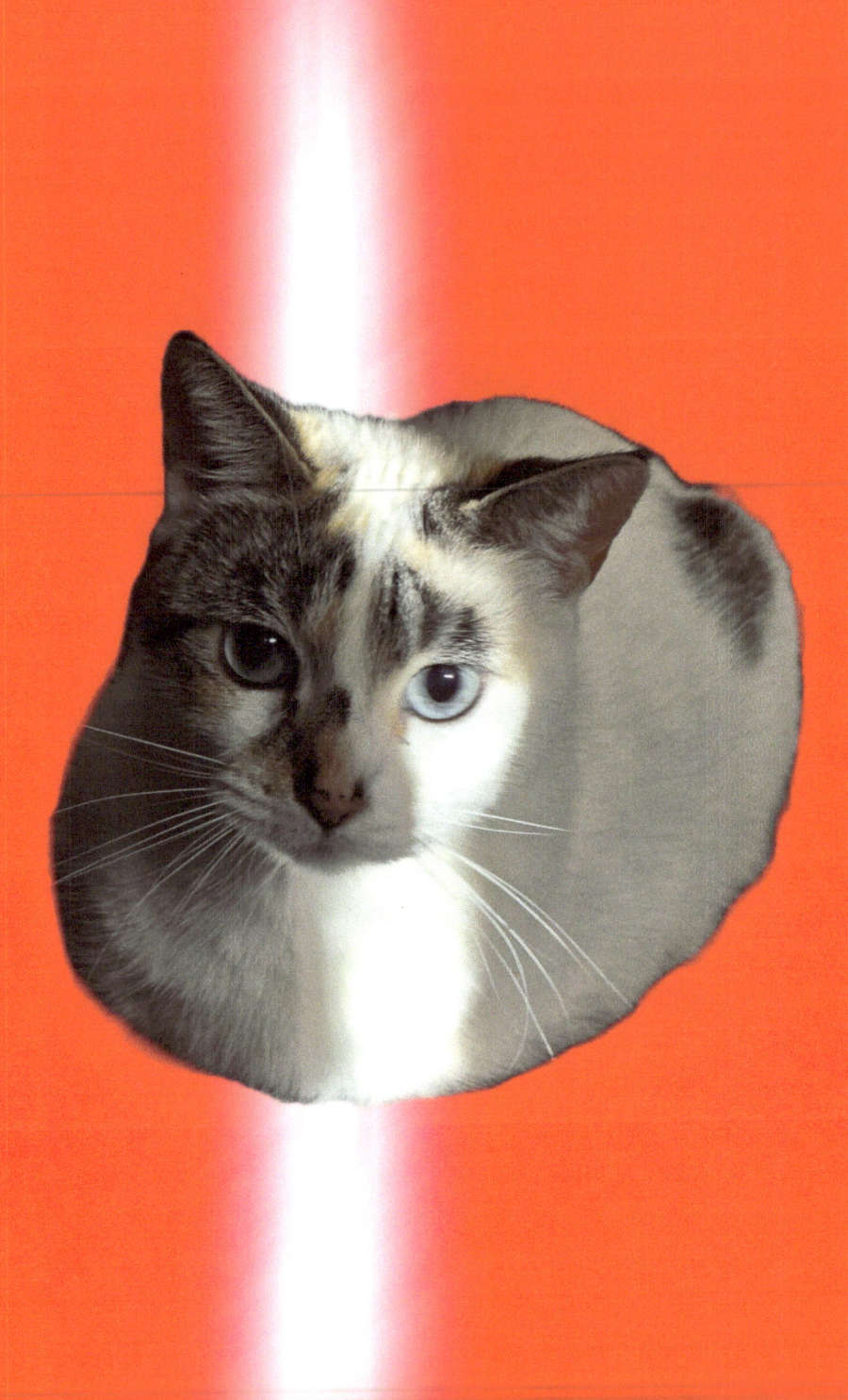

I DON'T KNOW
WHAT TO SAY FOR THIS NEXT
PART SO ILL LET CHRIS TALK
ABOUT IT IN THE NEXT PAGE
I GUESS....

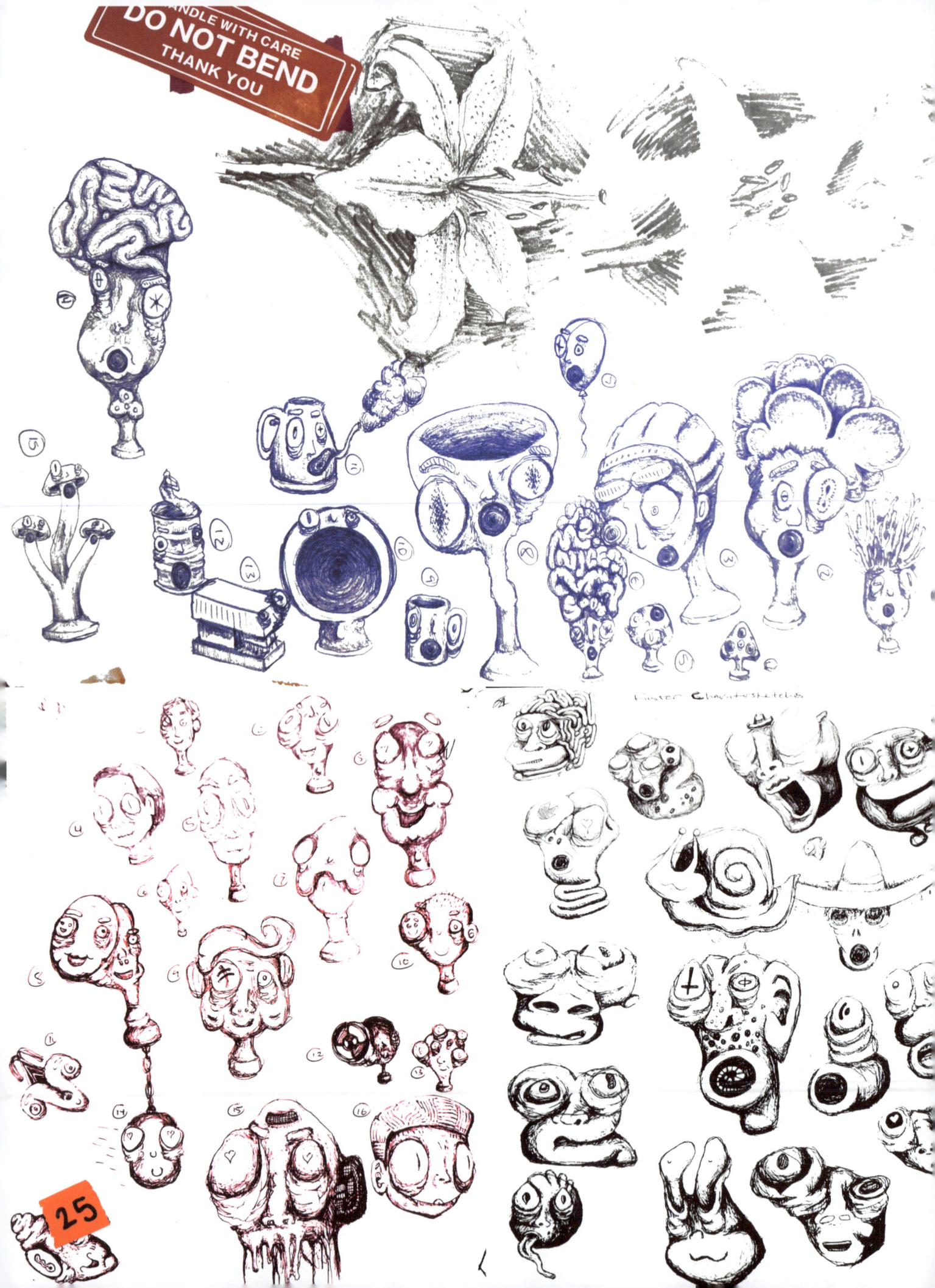

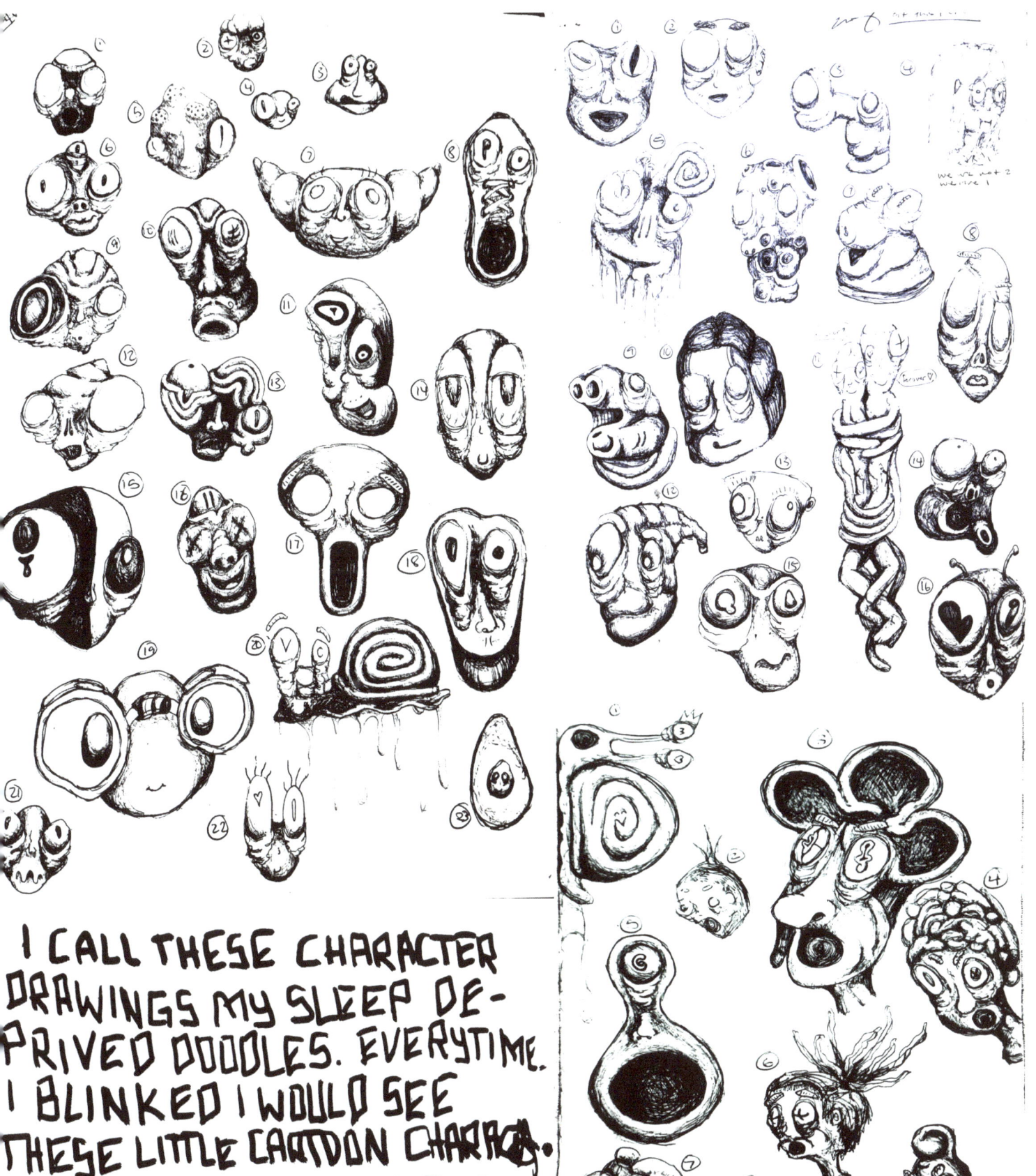

I CALL THESE CHARACTER DRAWINGS MY SLEEP DEPRIVED DOODLES. EVERYTIME I BLINKED I WOULD SEE THESE LITTLE CARTOON CHARACS. THESE TOOK ME SO LITTLE TO MAKE. THEY JUST KEPT POOPING OUT.

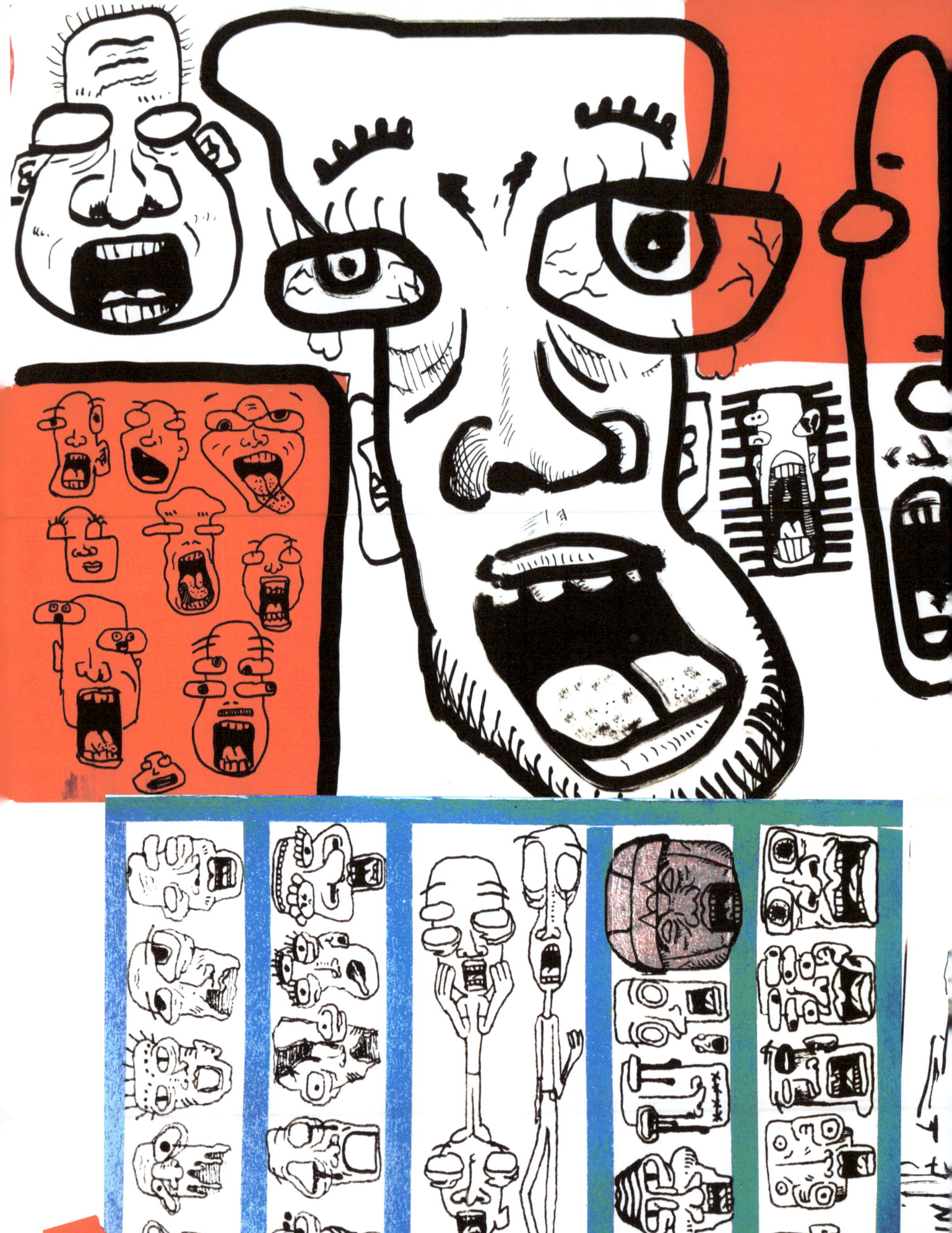

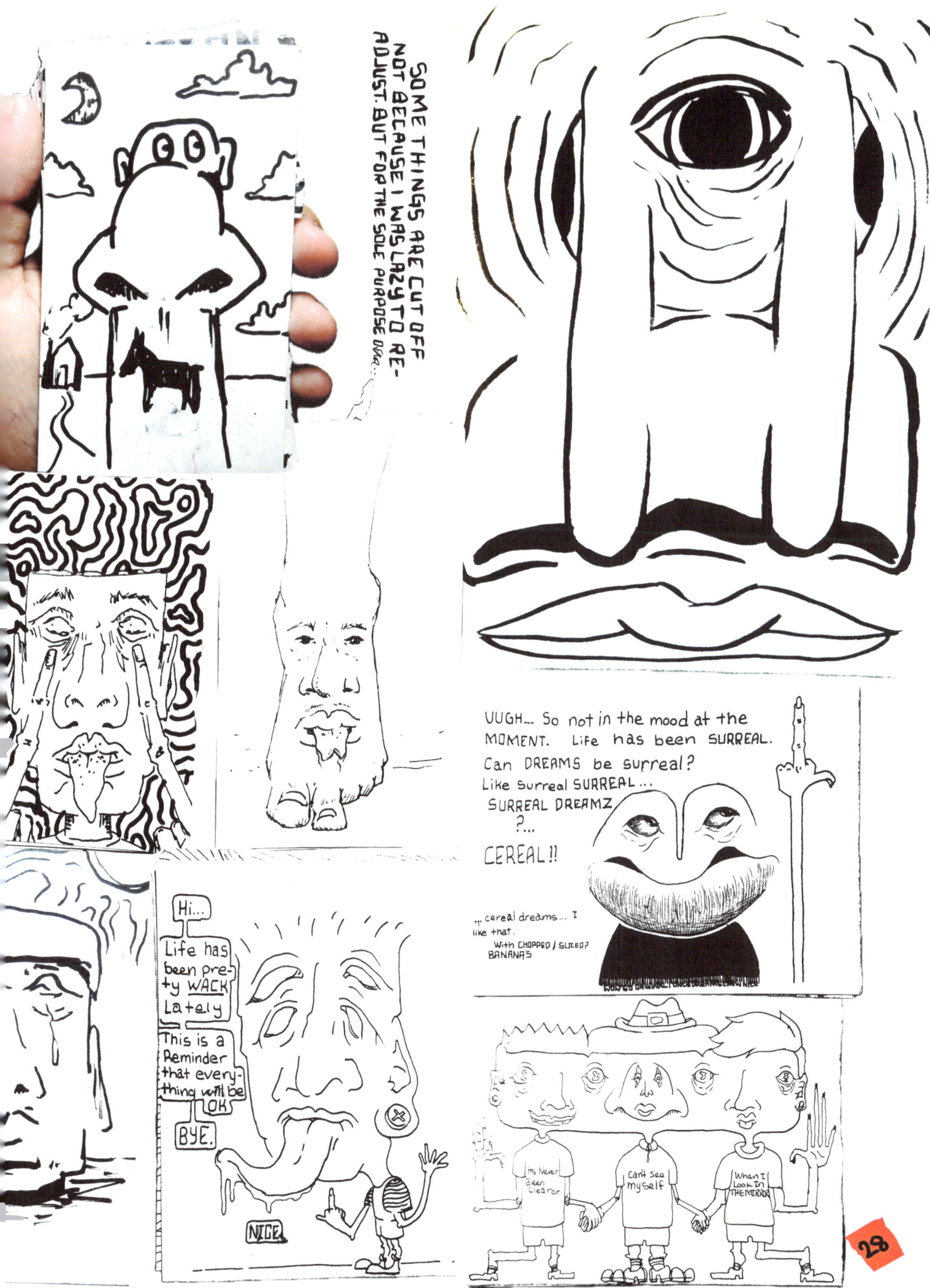

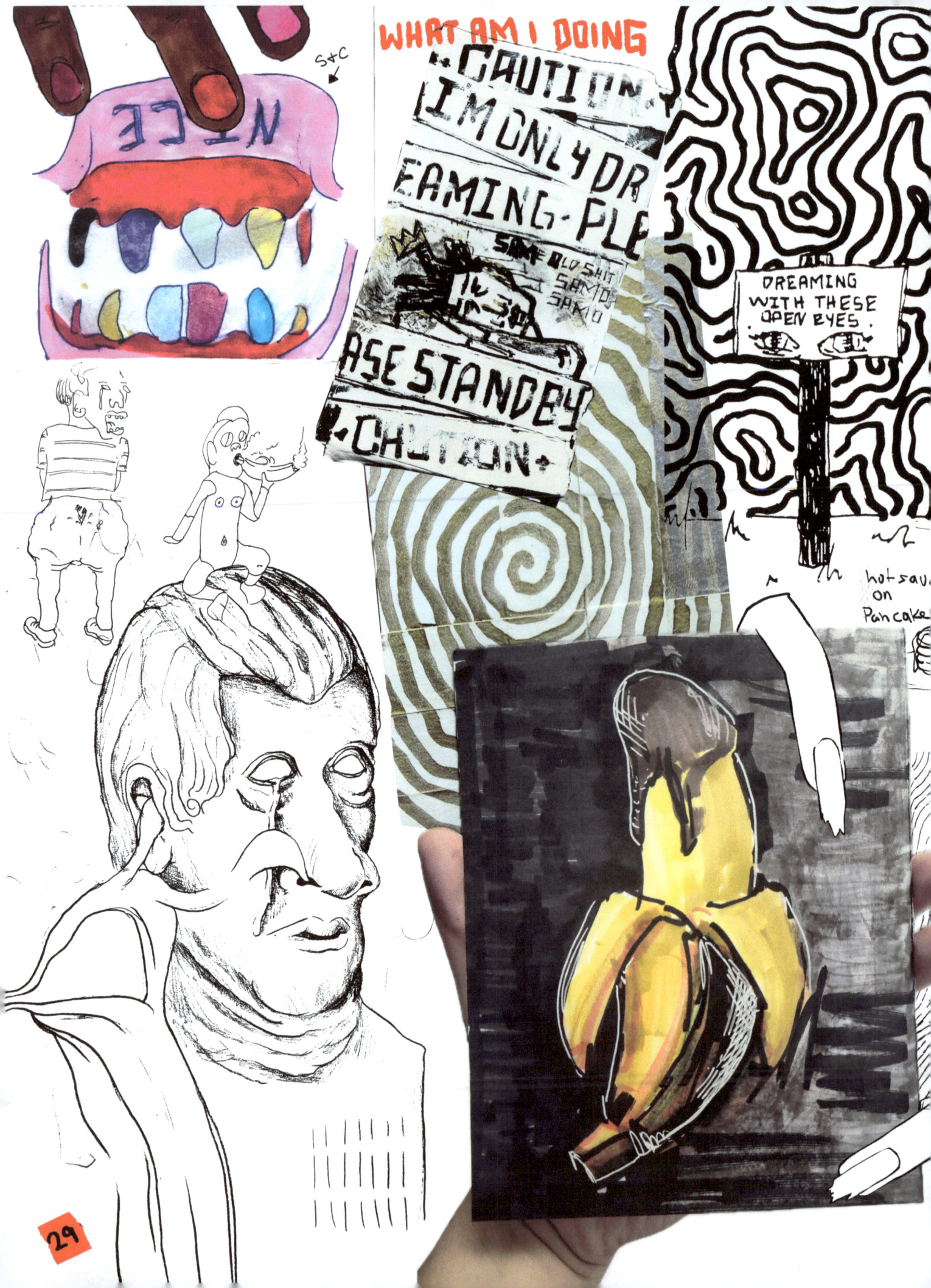

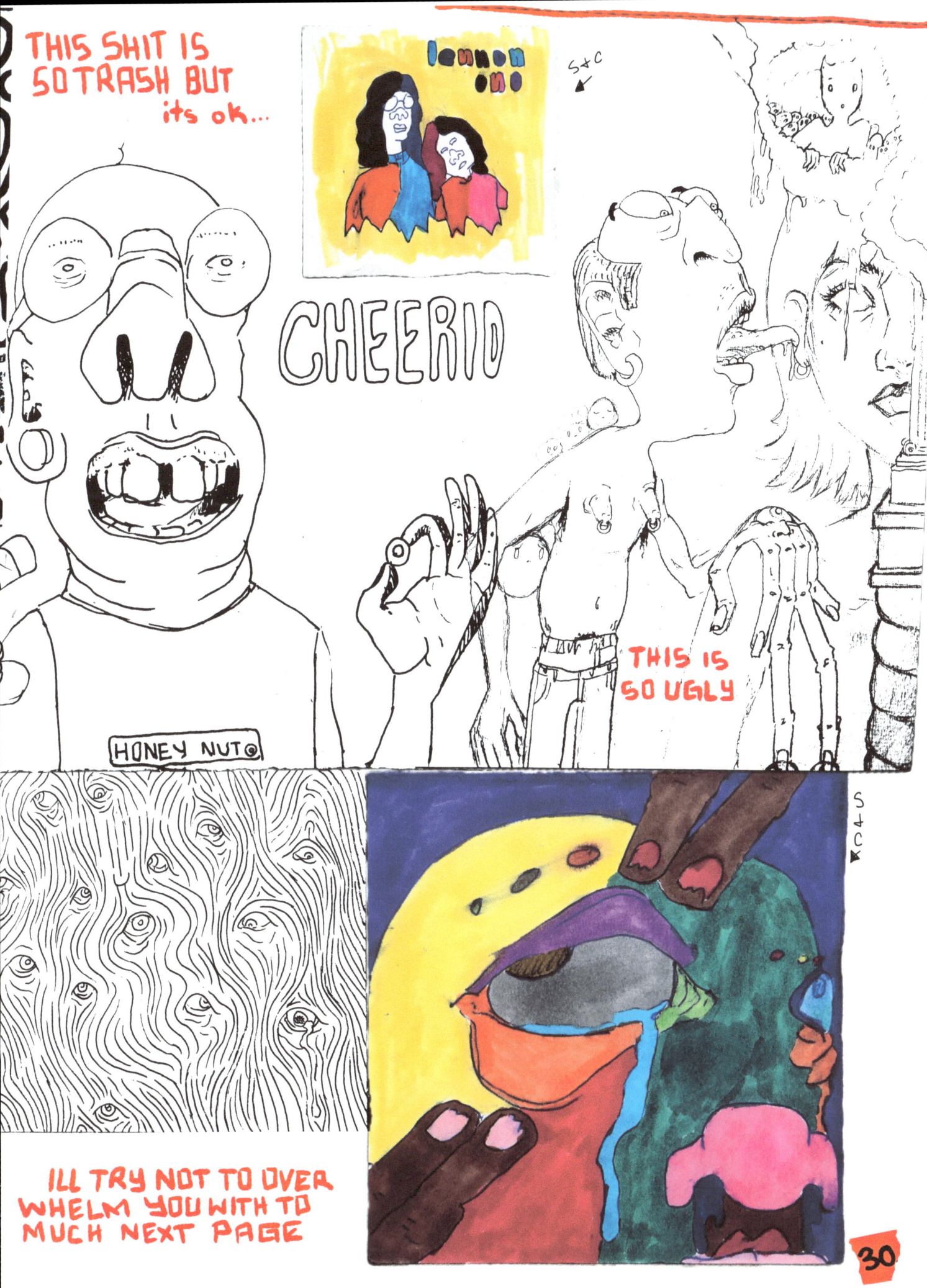

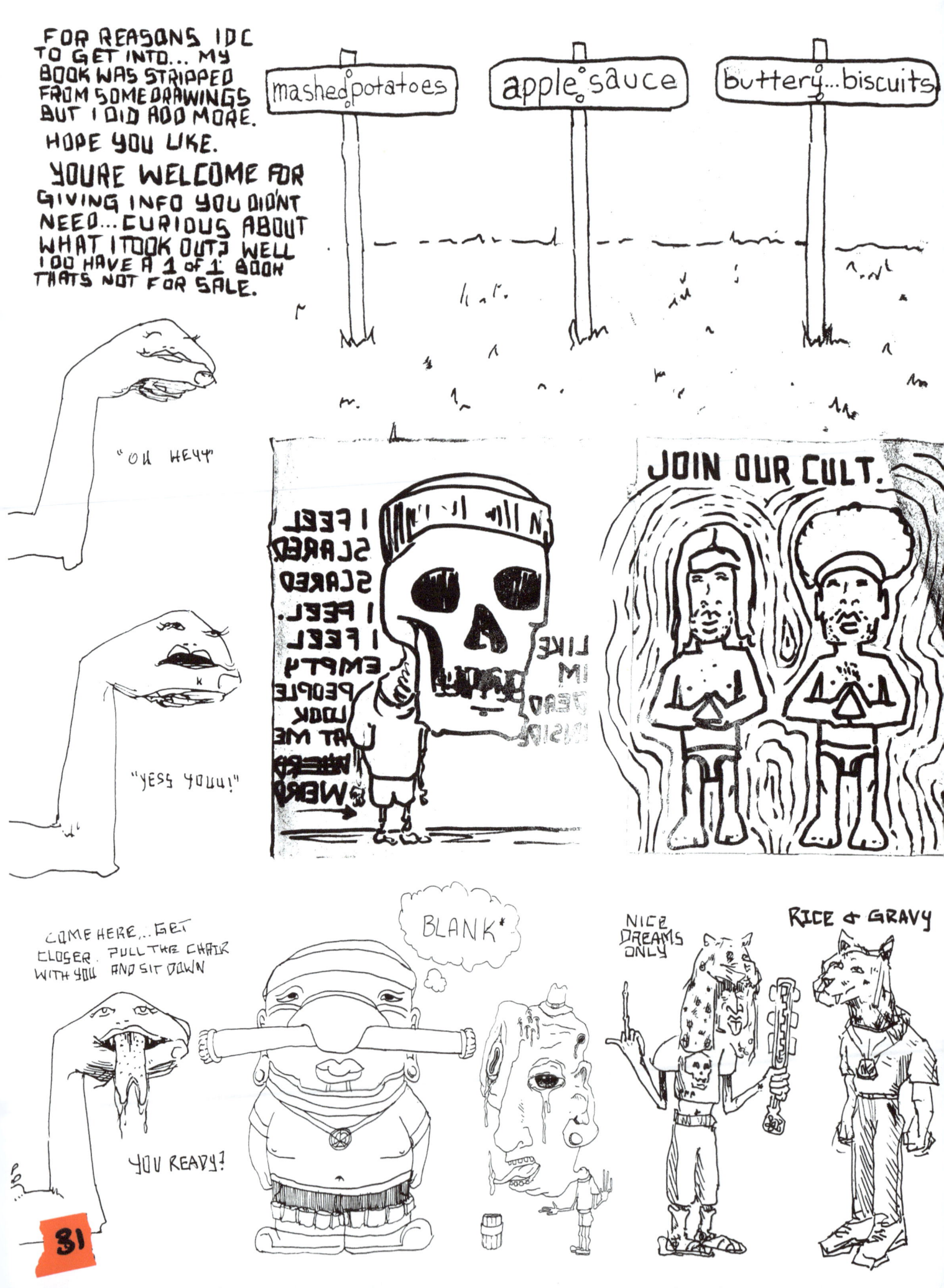

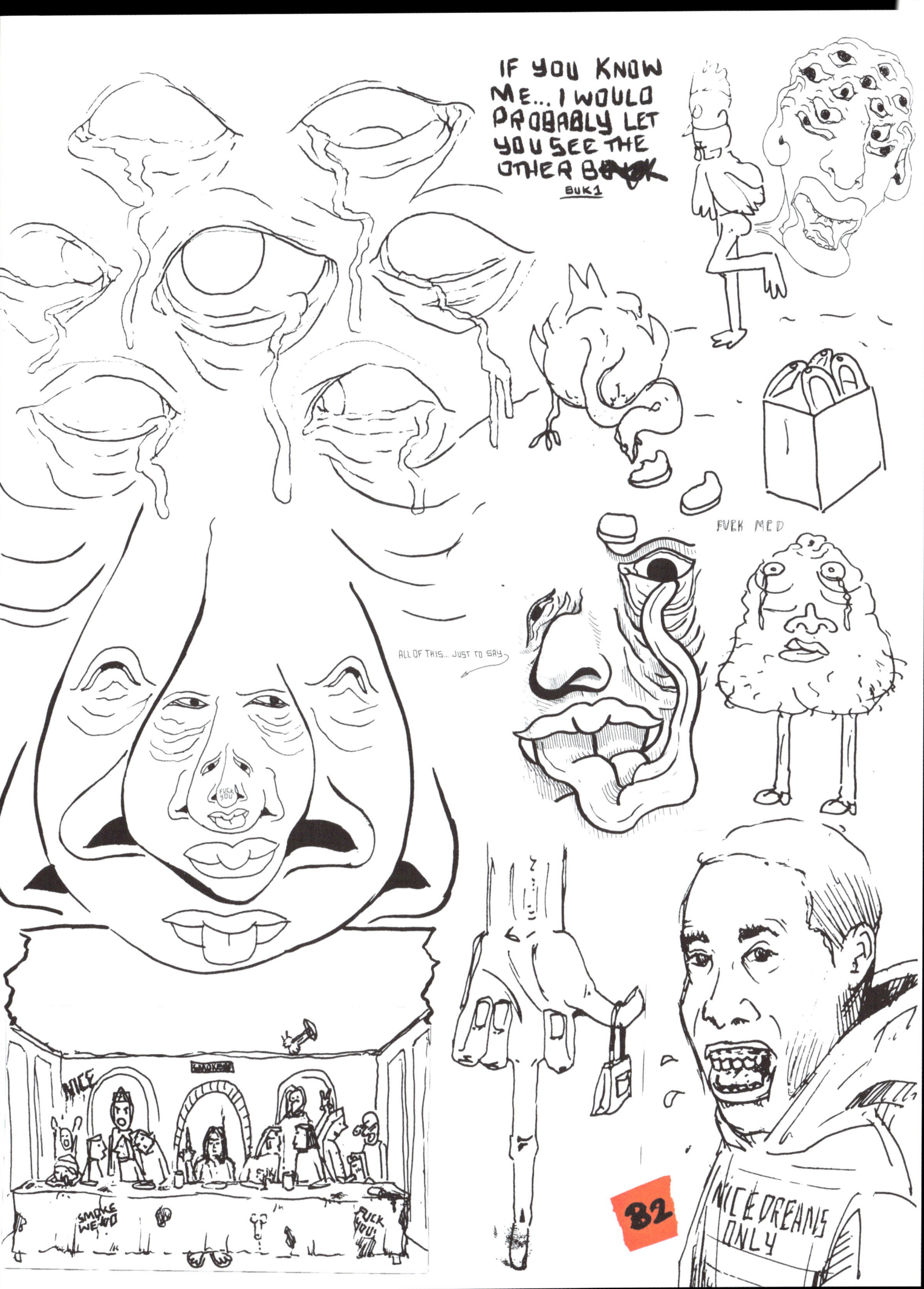

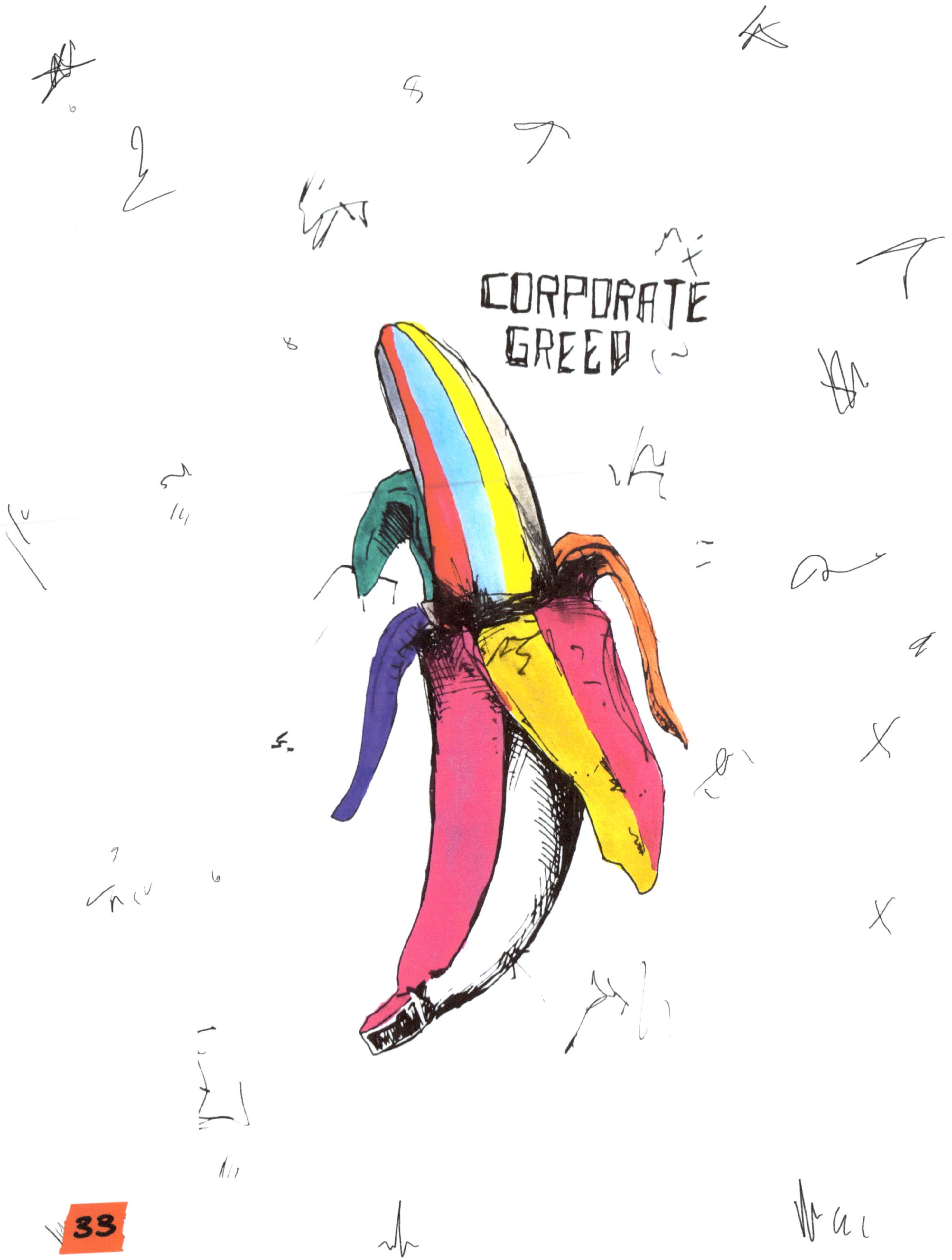

CORPORATE GREED

33

UP ABOVE IS A SEMAJHE & CHRIS COLLAB

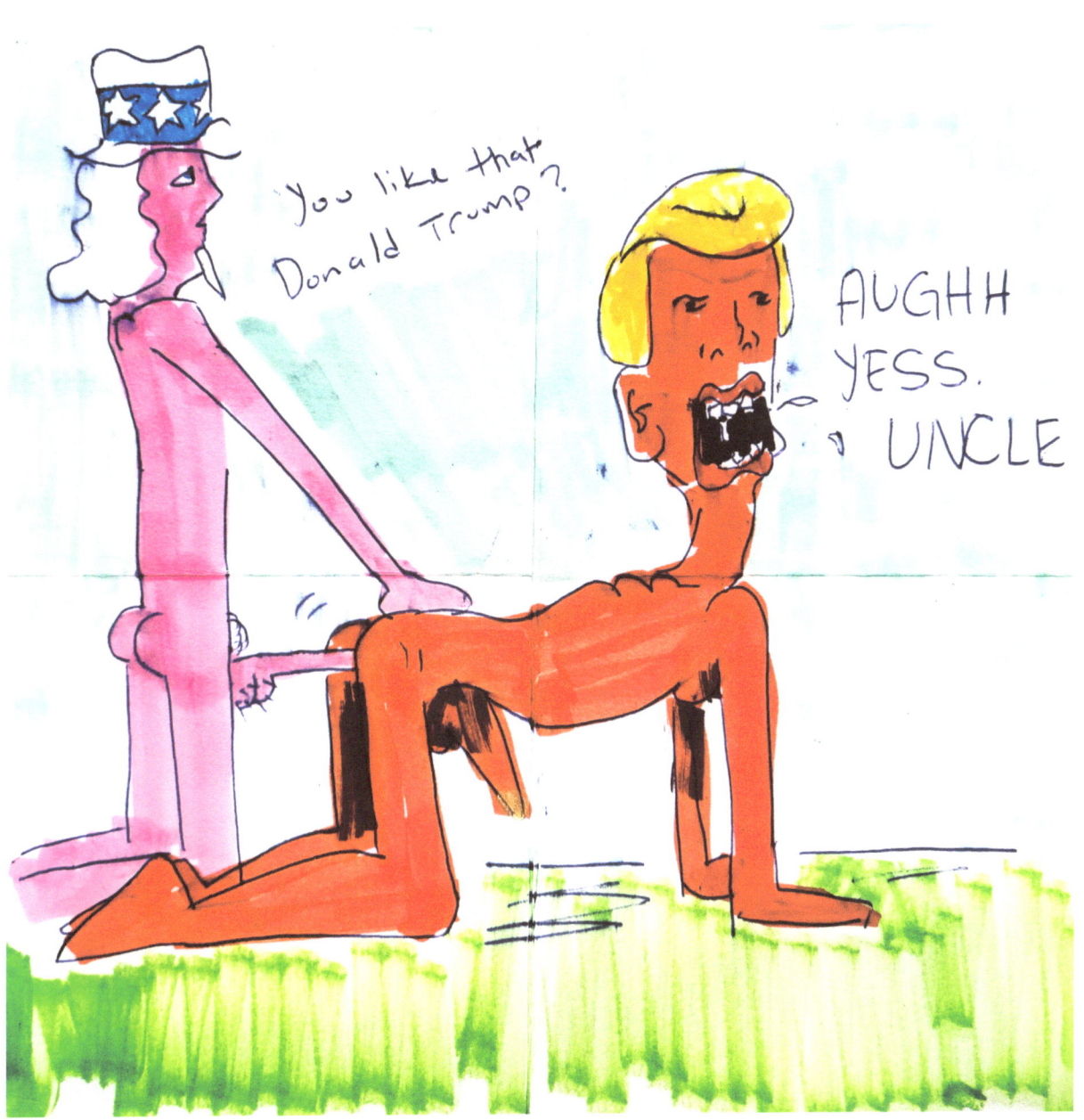

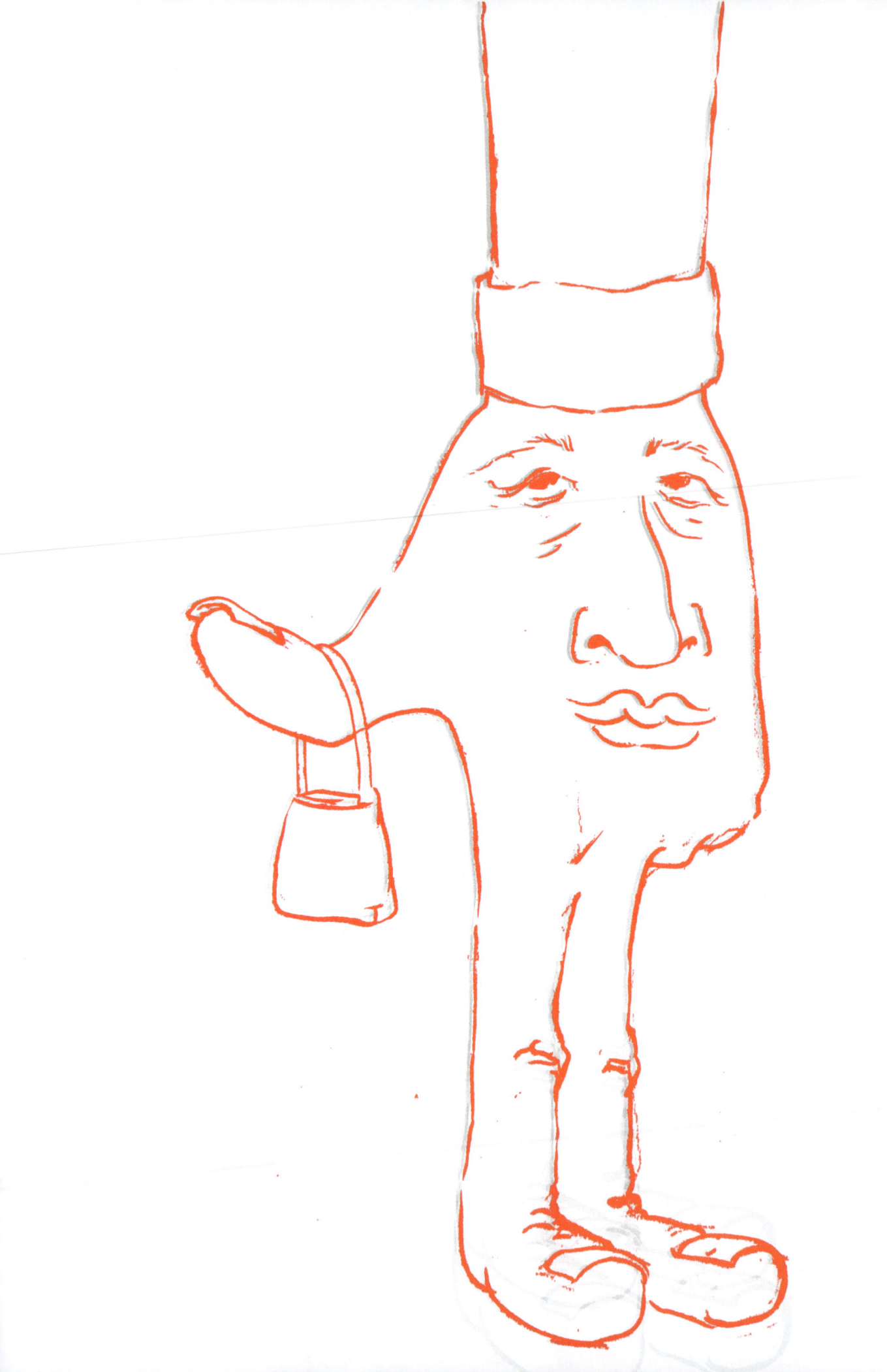

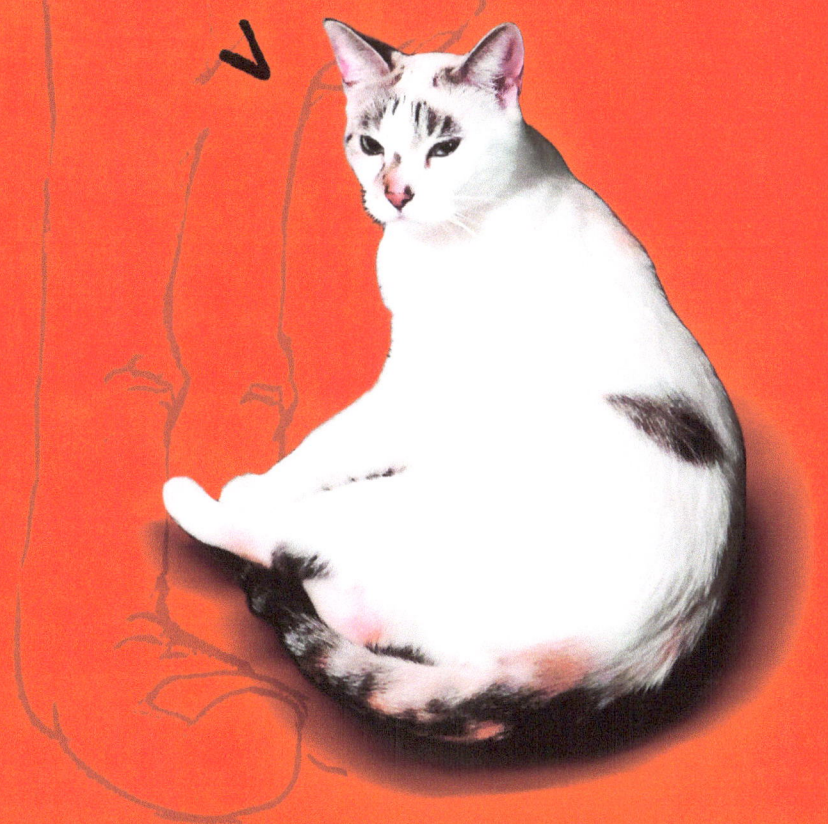

UGHH... YOU AGAIN?

WHY YOU BOTHERING ME... JUST TURN THE PAGE ALREADY. UNLIKE LAST TIME I'M NOT SURE ON WHAT WILL BE NEXT.
I'M OVER IT

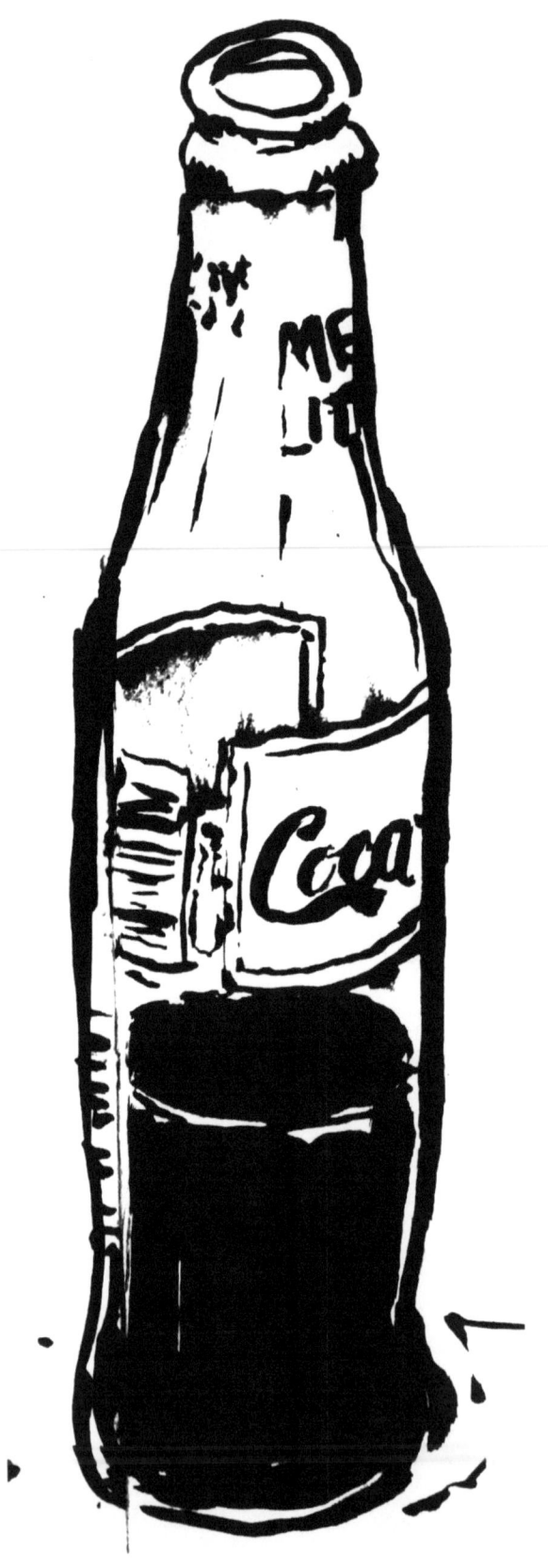

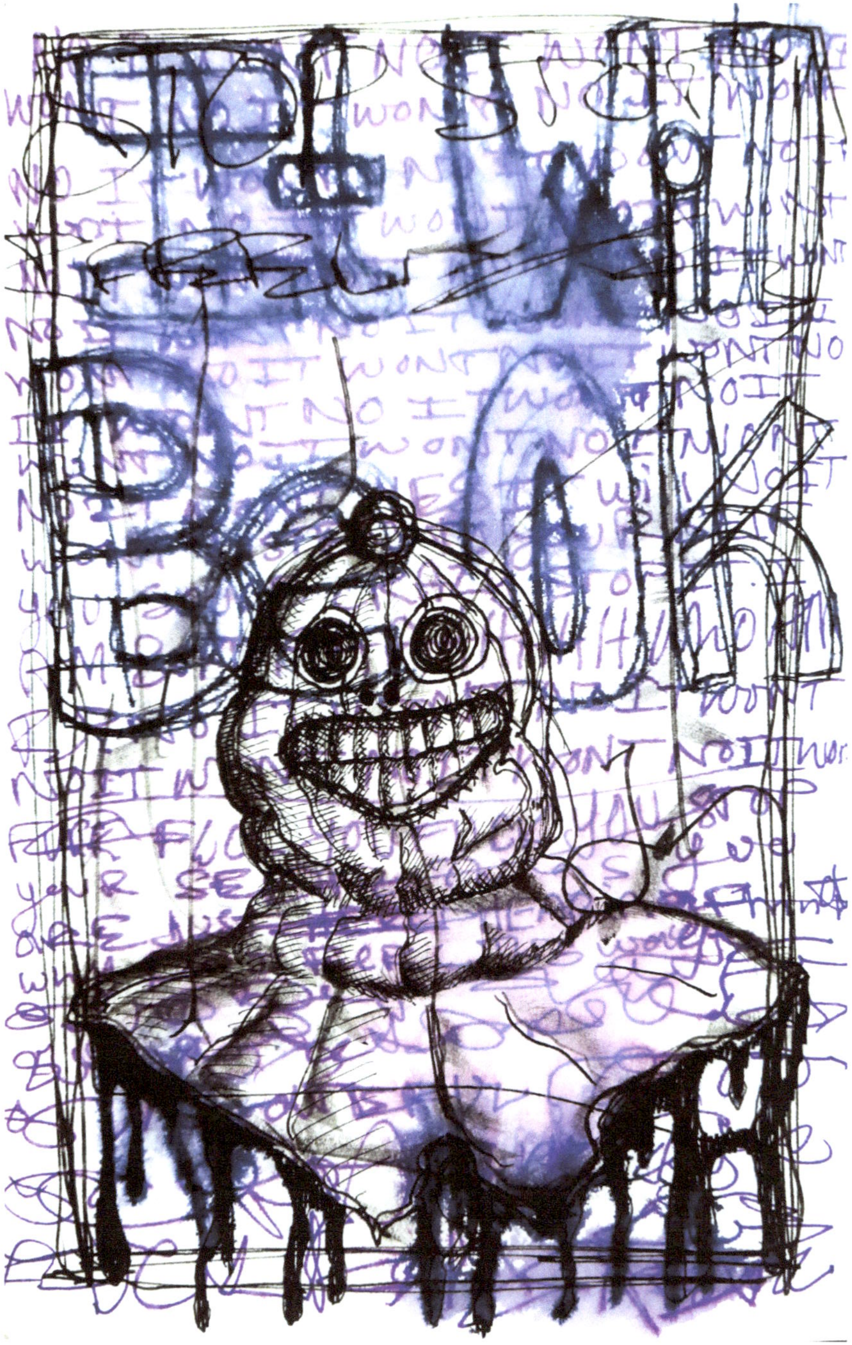

PRINT-TRANFER / WHAT EVER

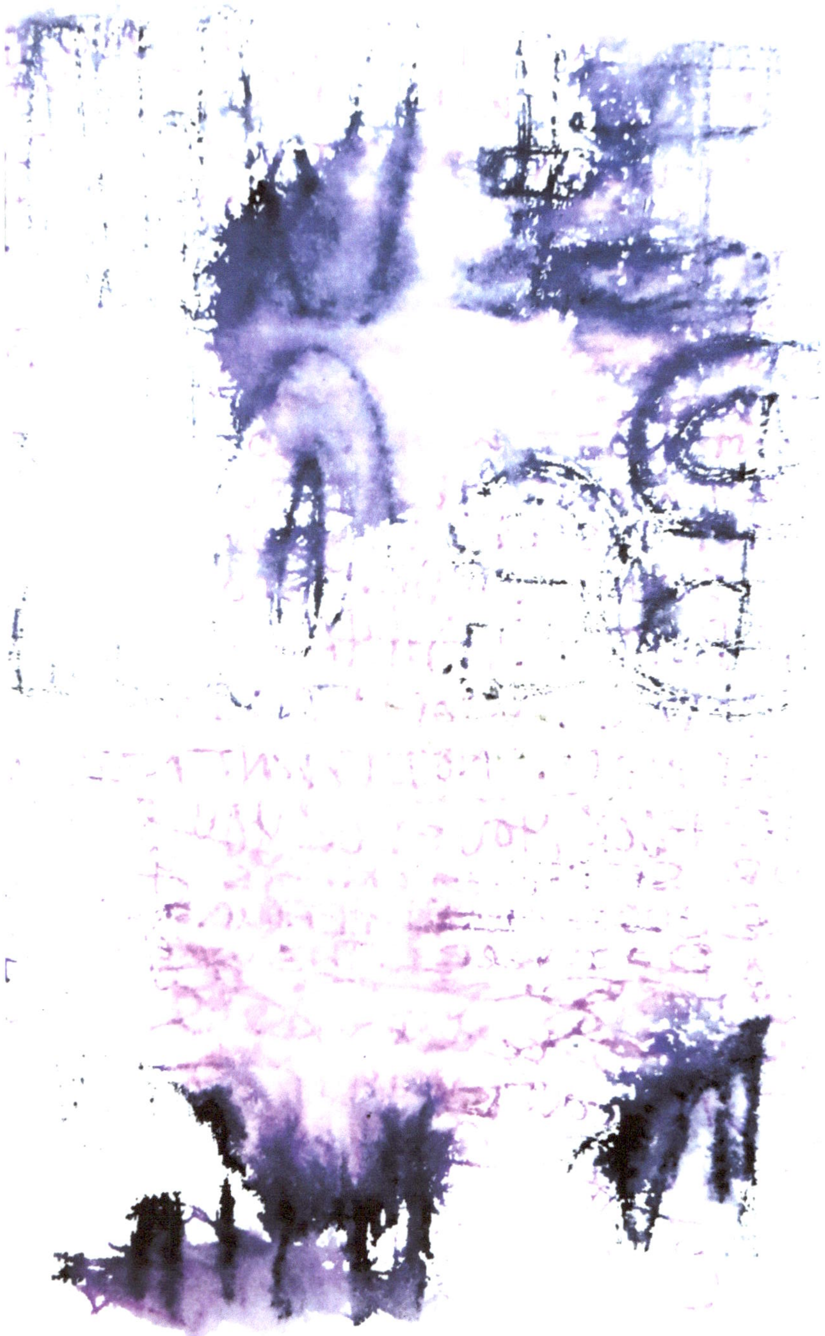

DRAWING

36

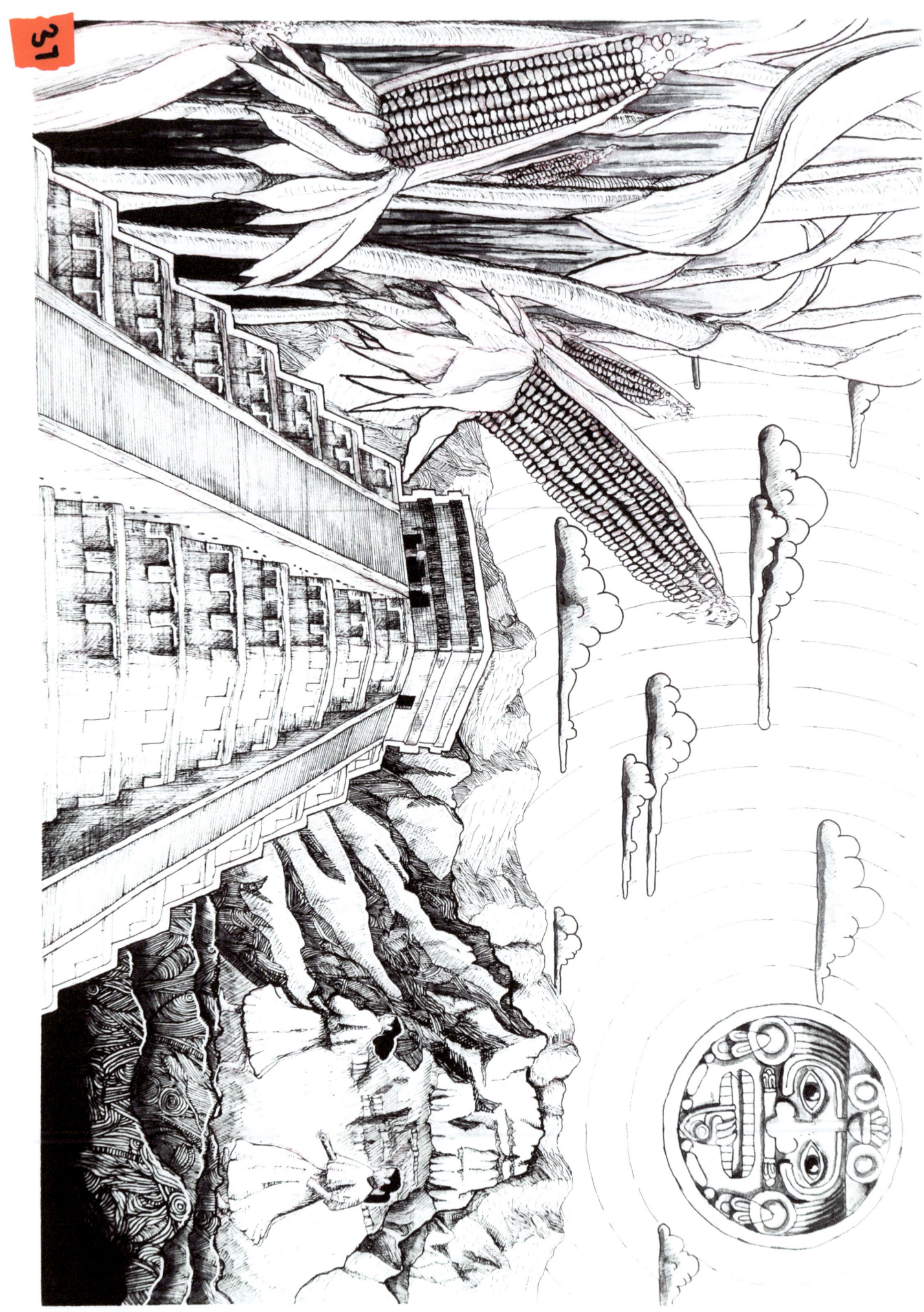

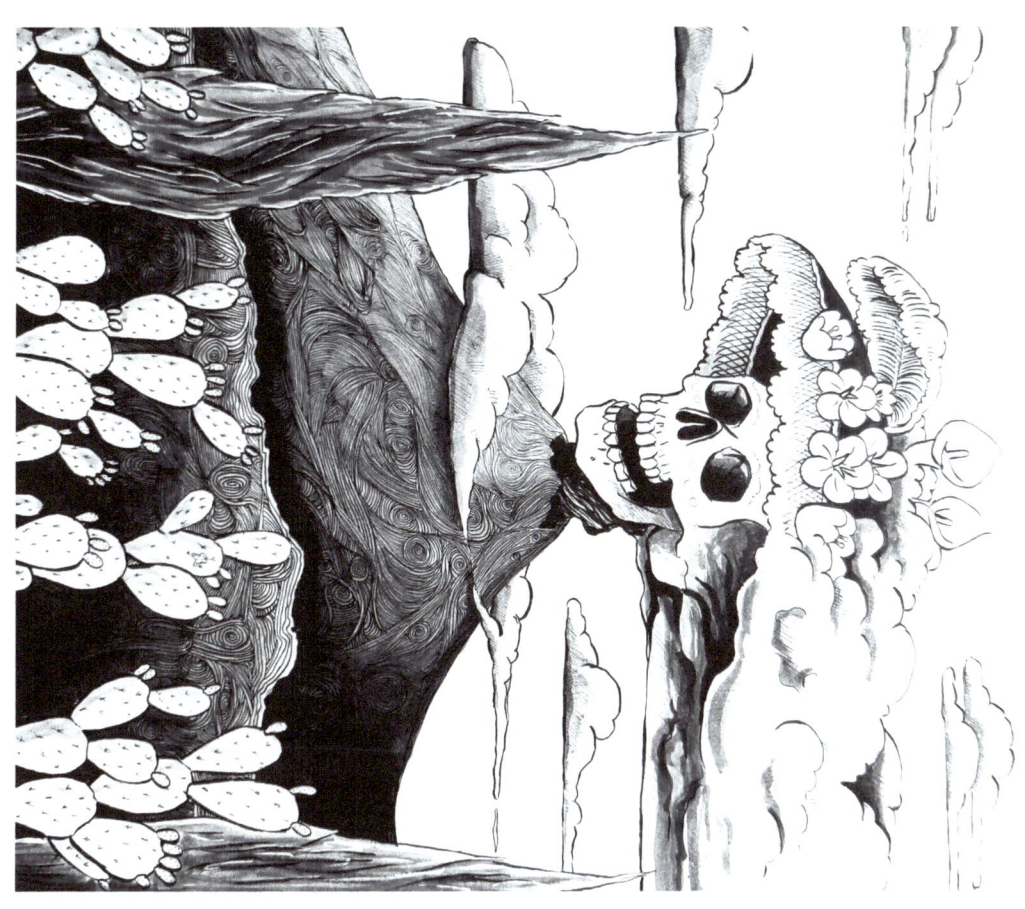
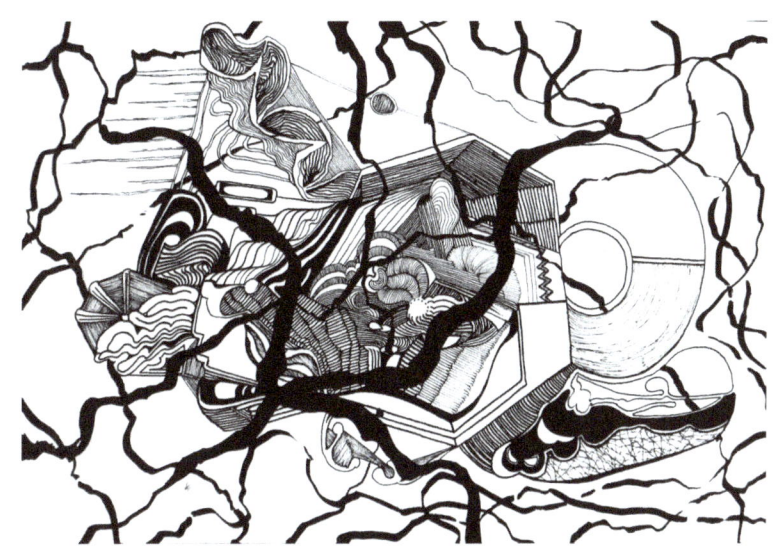

The constant questioning of "him".. ~~GOD~~
trying to grasp his hand, in hopes of being saved.
you failed me so many times. Just Left me to drown.
Lying to my self that everything will be ok.

My stomach is turning right now...
I just keep trembling. I don't know why.

Just feels like people want me to believe what
ever made up story some random dude said.
All that Religion has done is give an excuse for
mass killings for not believing in the same shit.

FUCK YOUR RELIGION

Practice on your own time &
Don't force it upon me and we are cool
Liberation for all.

FUCK WAR. FUCK CORPORATE GREED.

LOVE YOUR NEIGHBOR.

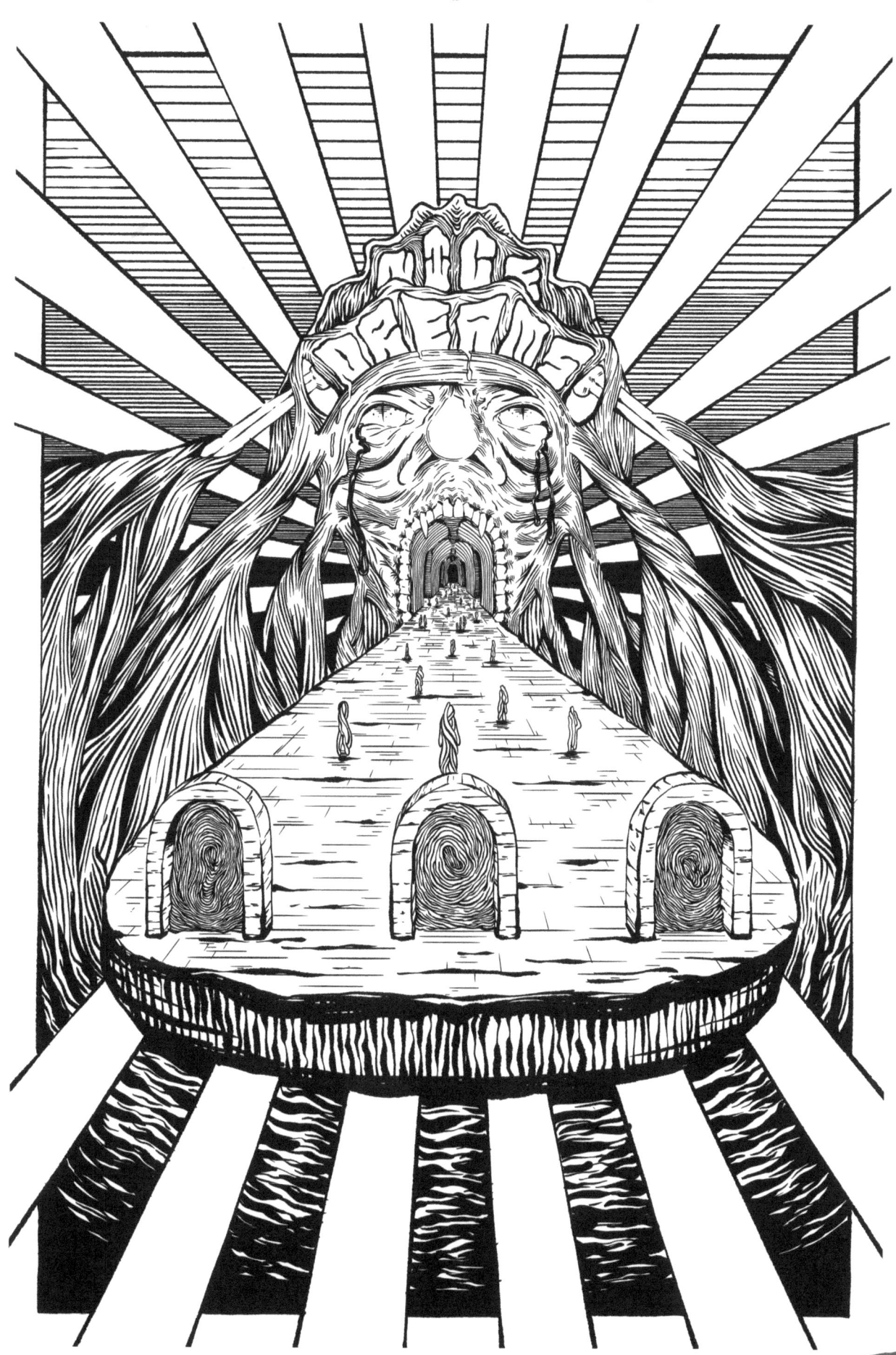

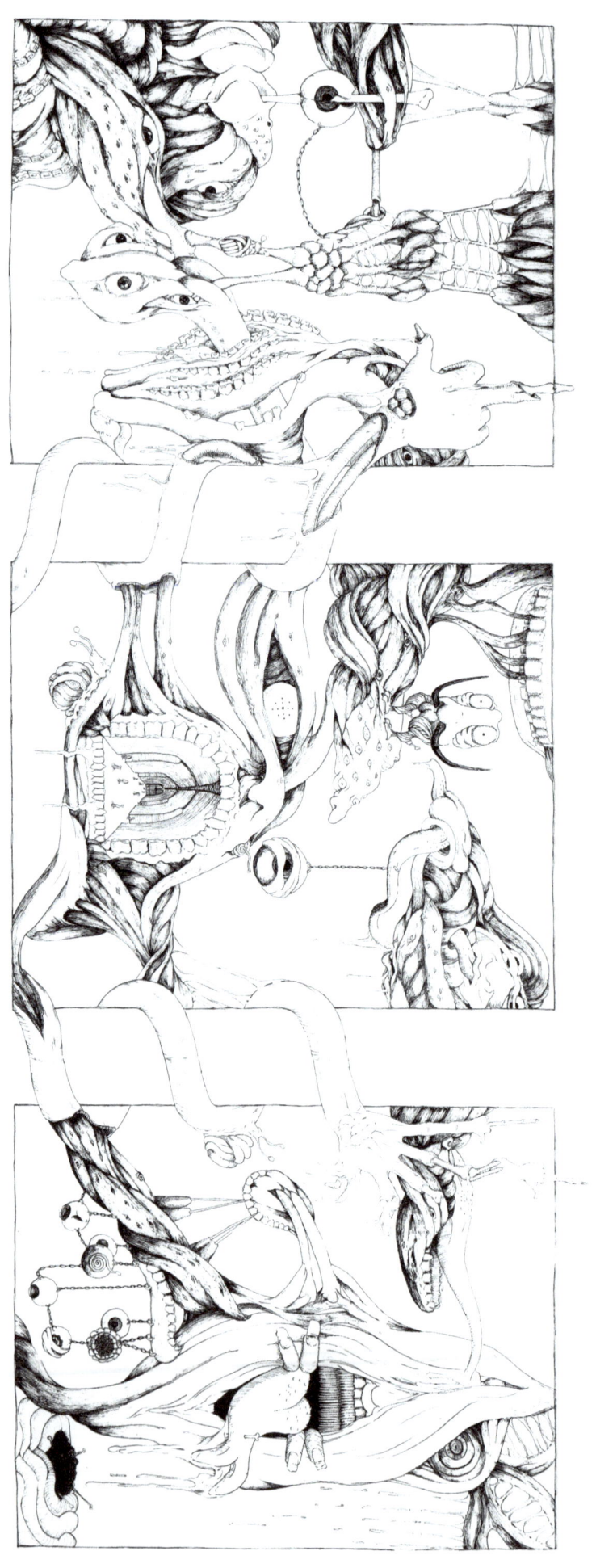

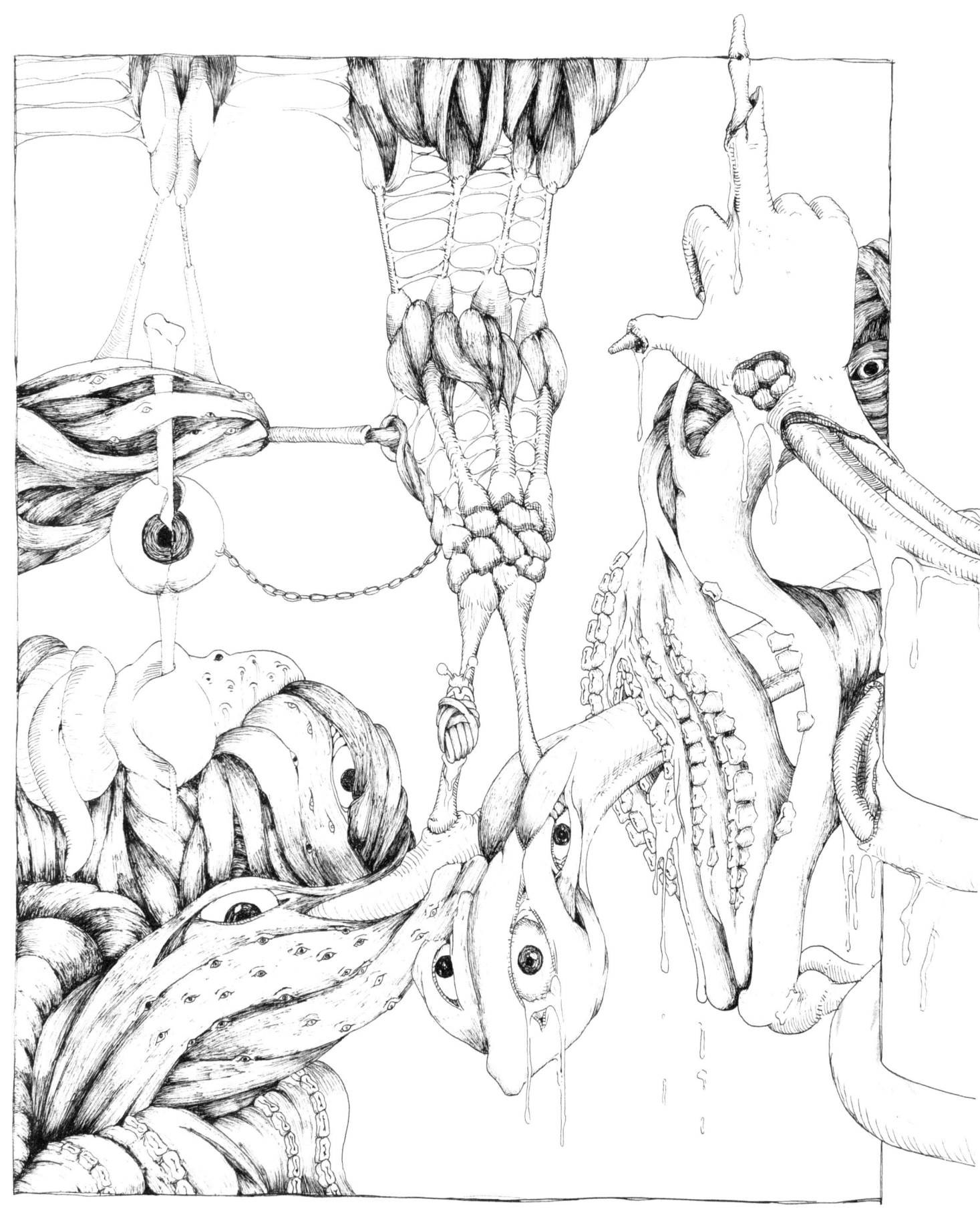

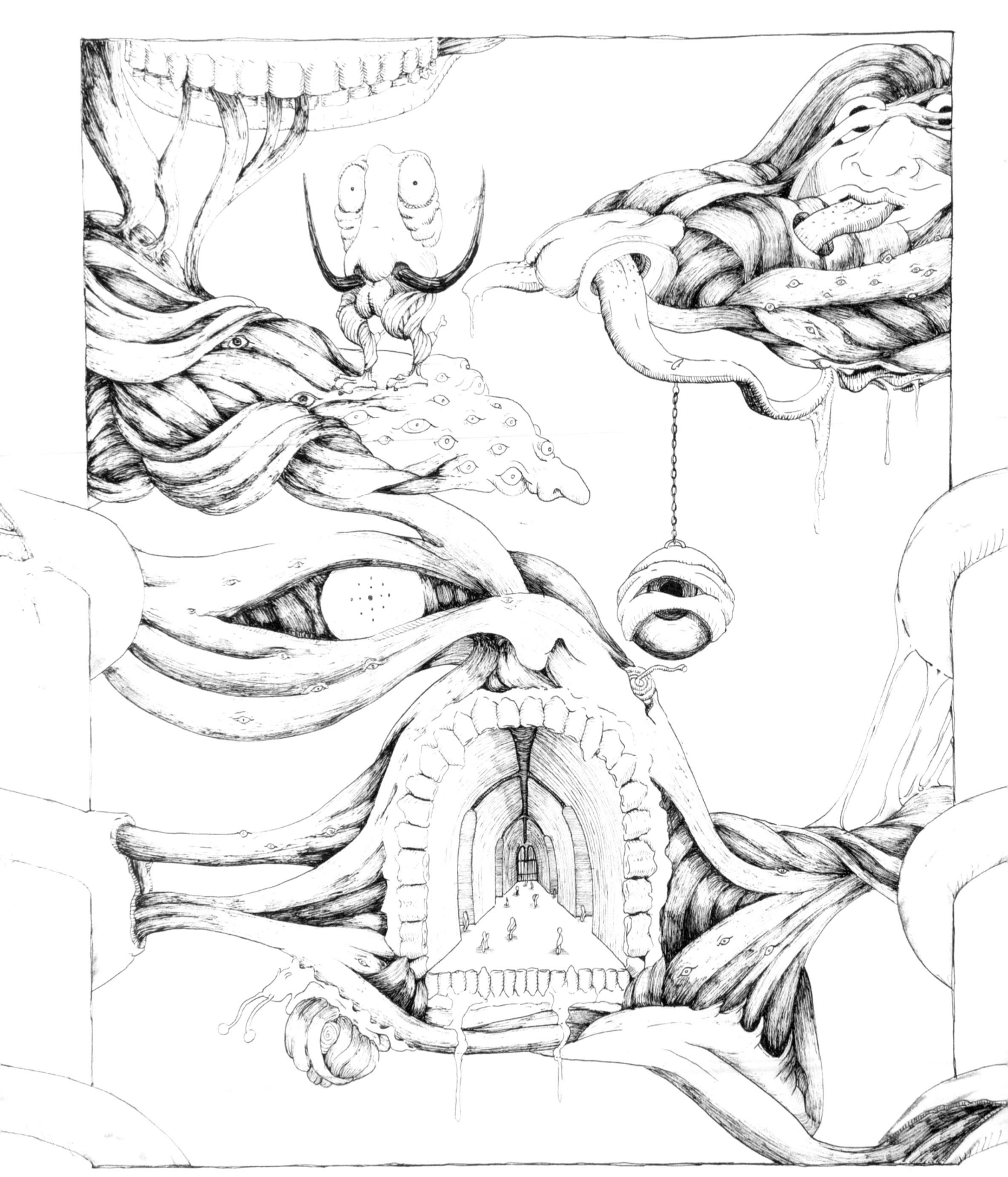

DREAMS

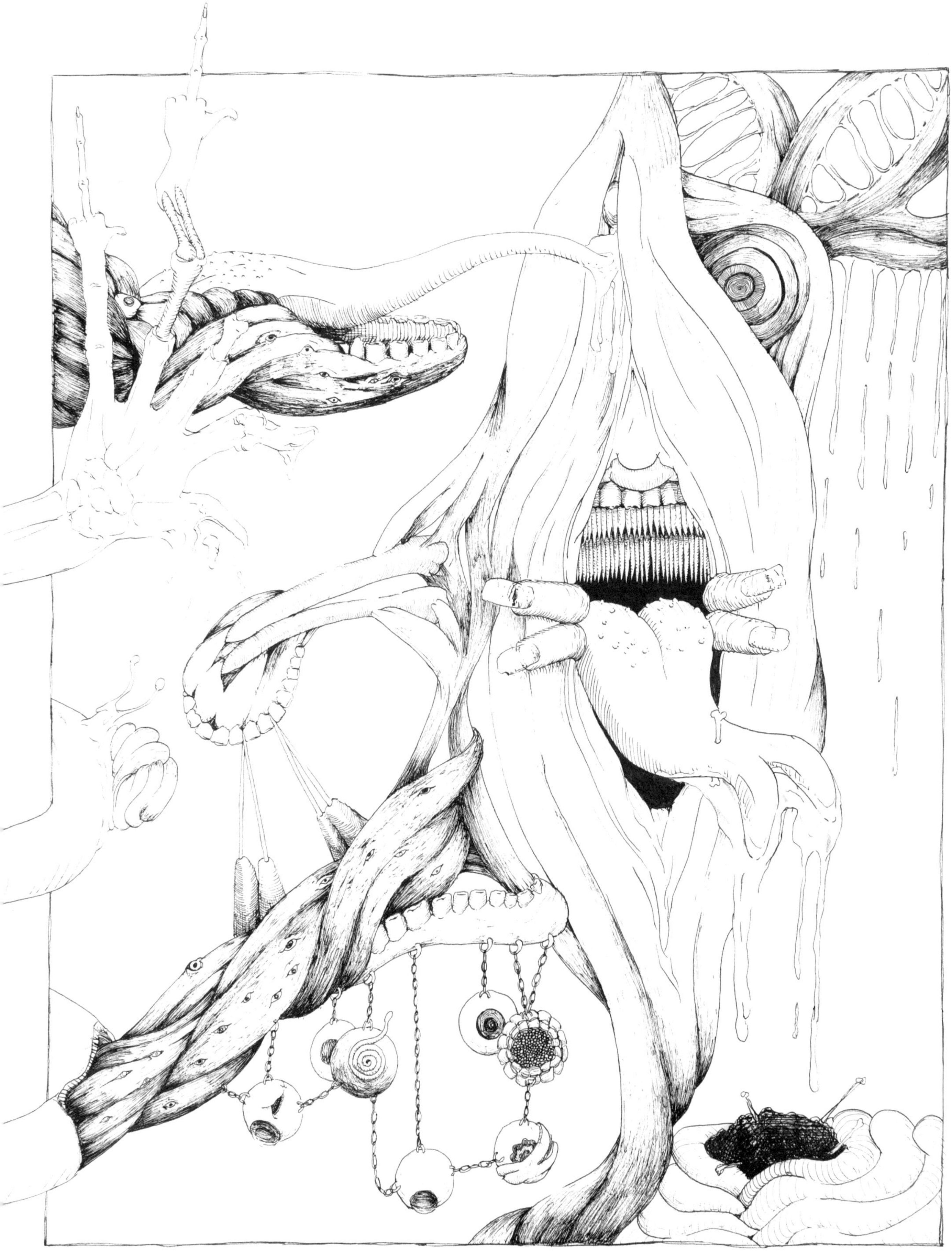

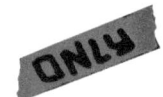

I WANT TO SAY THANK YOU TO EVERY SINGLE PERSON WHO HAS SUPPORTED ME. I LOVE AND APPRECIATE YOU SO MUCH.

MY IMMEDIATE FAMILY.
MY CLOSE FRIENDS
TEACHERS WHO HAVE WENT THE EXTRA MILE.

I WON'T PUT DOWN NAMES BUT YOU KNOW WHO YOU ARE

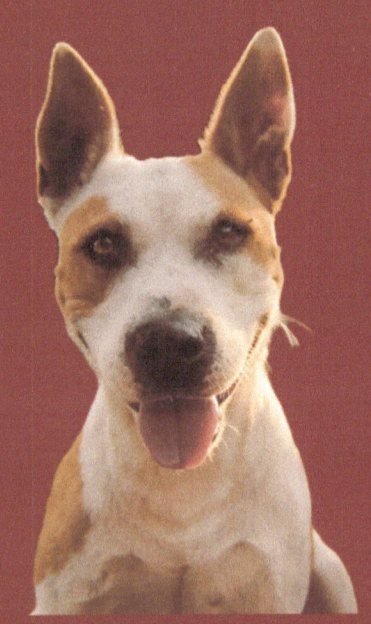 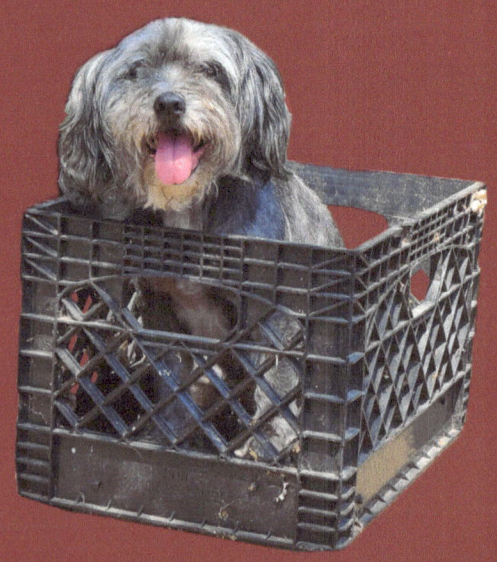

ZEPHYR WAS SO LOVING TO ANYONE SHE MET. LOVED HUGS + KISSES. ALWAYS GREETED WITH HER PAW FOR A HANDSHAKE. MY FIRST DOG. HAS BEEN THERE MOST OF MY LIFE. I MISS YOU SO MUCH.

NOT THE BEST FOTO OF BABE BUT CAPTURES HIS INNER CAT
LOVE BOXES. GETTING IN THE WAY. I MISS YOU.. YOU WERE SO MUCH FUN. COULD ALWAYS RELY ON YOU TO MAKE ME LAUGH.

IN HONOR OF MY 2 FRIENDS, FAM, PETS.
ZEPHYR + BABE
WE WILL MEET AGAIN IN THE NEXT 80 YEARS THE YALL CAN HELP ME OUT WHEN I'M OLD

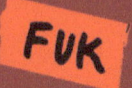

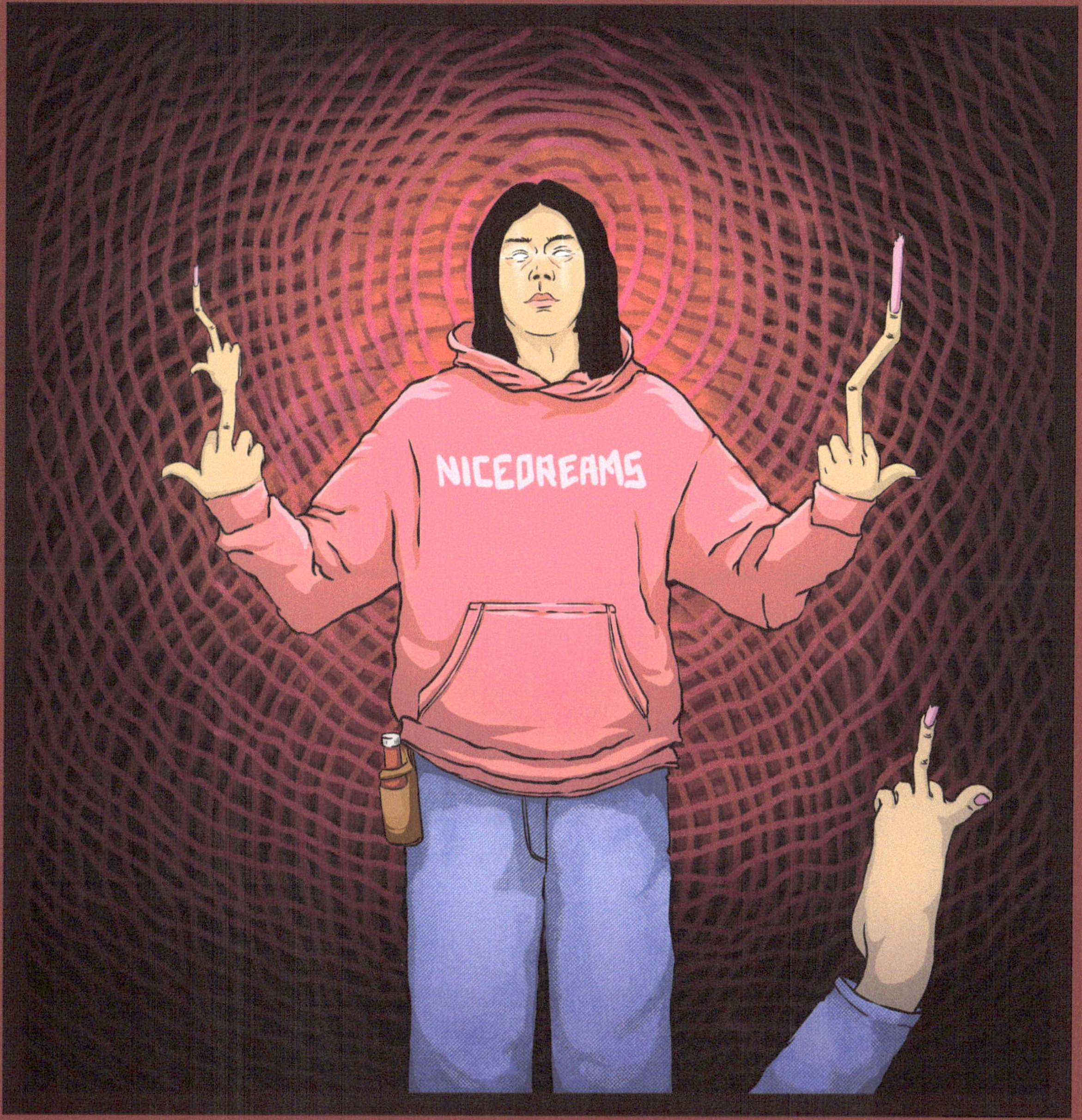

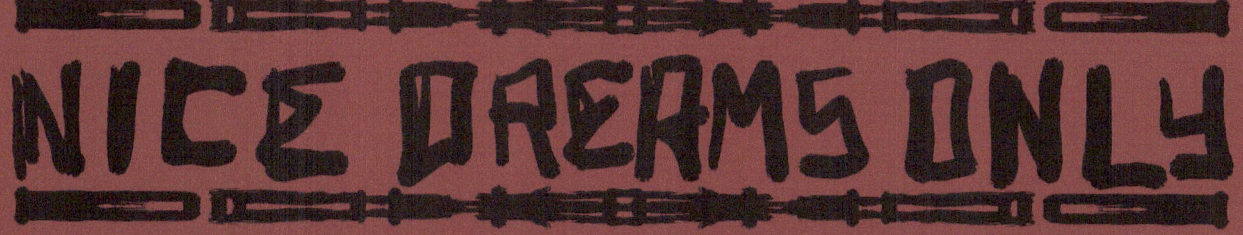

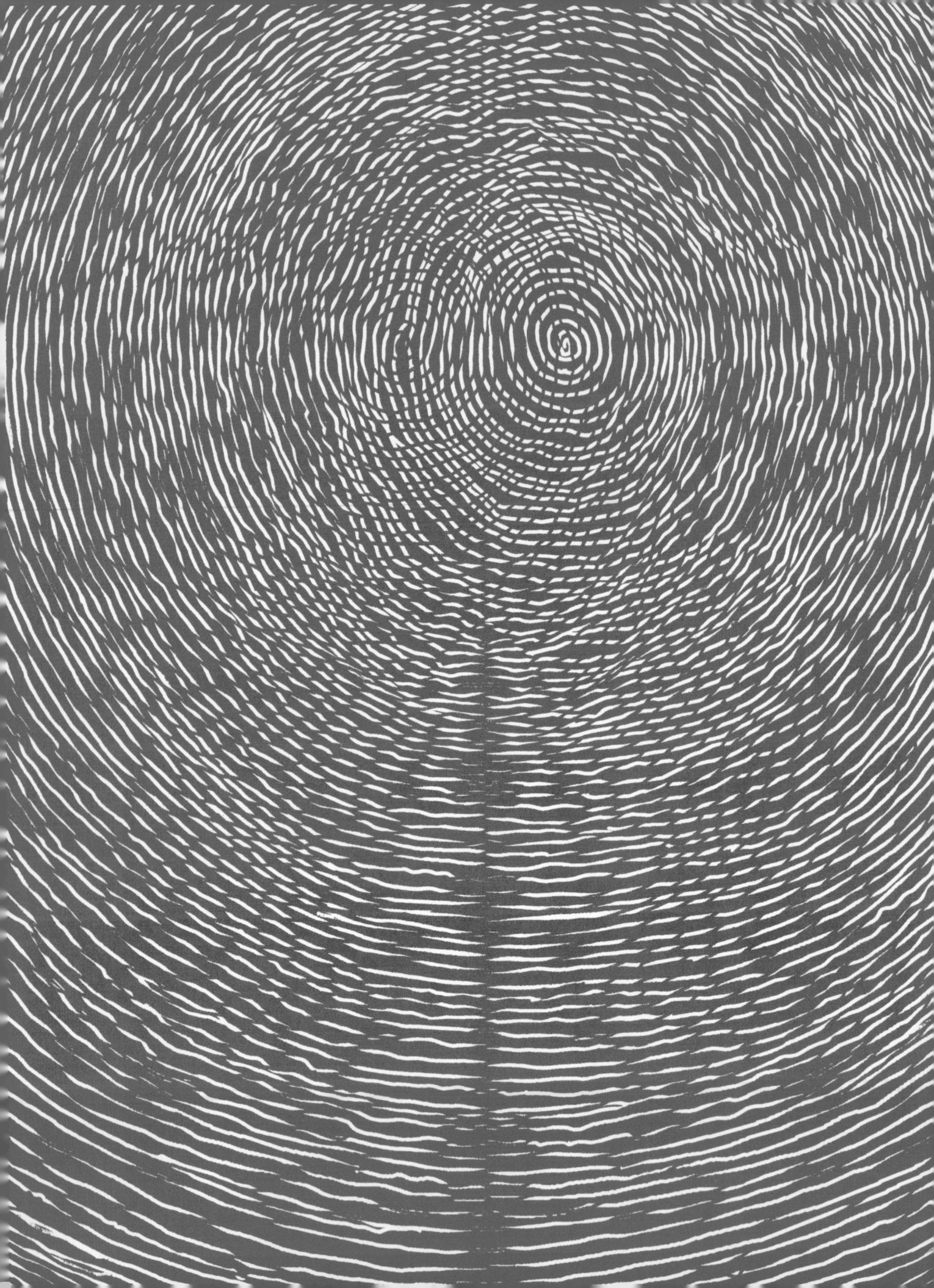

YOU BITCH!!
YOU THOUGHT YOU CAN LEAVE WITHOUT SAYING GOODBYE?

I'LL REMEMBER THAT FOR NEXT TIME.

GOOD YOU'RE LEAVING I WAS GETTING TIRED OF LOOKING AT YOUR UNFLATTERING FACE FROM DOWN HERE. NO WONDER WHY YOU TAKE SELFIES FROM A HIGHER ANGLE YOU BOYSENBERRY. UNSEASONED BOILED CHICKEN. SOME HOW BURNING IT AND IT STILL RAW INSIDE.
LEAVE!

Pussy

HOT SAUCE ON PANCAKES

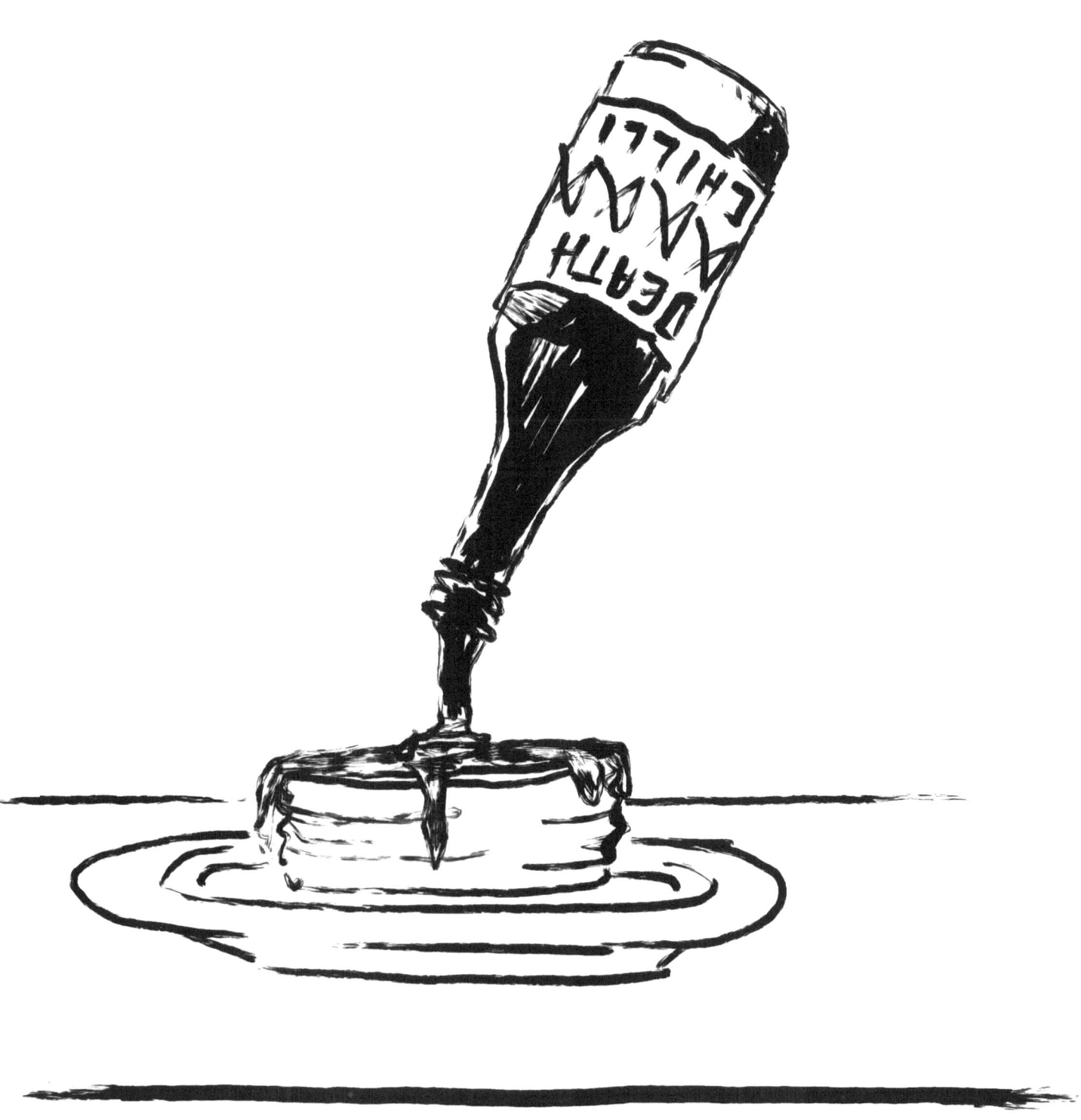

www.ingramcontent.com/pod-product-compliance
Lightning Source LLC
Chambersburg PA
CBHW051213220526
45473CB00003B/1011